Guatemala's Political Puzzle

Guatemala's Political Puzzle

Georges A. Fauriol
and
Eva Loser

Transaction Books
New Brunswick (USA) and Oxford (UK)

Library of Congress Catalog Number: 88-1885
ISBN 0-88738-213-4
Printed in the United States of America

LIBRARY OF CONGRESS
Library of Congress Cataloging-in-Publication Data

Fauriol, Georges A.
    Guatemala's political puzzle / Georges A. Fauriol and Eva Loser.
        p.   cm.
    Bibliography: p.
    Includes index.
    ISBN 0-88738-213-4
    1. Guatemala—Politics and government—1945–1985.
2. Guatemala—Politics and government—1985–
I. Loser, Eva, 1962–
II. Title.
F1466.5.F38   1988
320.97281—dc19   88-1885
                                                                    CIP

Contents

Preface

The airplane engine roars and strains. Just below, rugged mountains, a few paths, no roads, and from time to time signs of habitation appear. Sitting in the copilot's seat, the approach to La Aurora airport of Guatemala City suddenly reveals an expansive metropolis. The city is built up, but the surrounding view is green with pines and other temperate vegetation due to the fact that this is a roughly 5,000-foot plateau encircled by mountains. In the distance, seemingly planted abruptly at the end of the airport runway, are high-peaked volcanoes actively emitting plumes of smoke. Closing in, the nose of the plane lines itself up with Avenida 6 in the center of town, and skirts at a low altitude over the older and crowded portions of the city. When La Aurora airport was first built, it was on the southern edge of town; urban growth has since caught up with it.

At decreasing speed, recognizable structures begin to appear on the left and below—the imposing greenish presidential palace, the modernistic Banco de Guatemala structure, the miniature Eiffel Tower-like Reformer's Tower, and the crowded and narrow downtown streets. Finally, the plane rolls down the runway and Guatemala City's surprisingly modern skyline of ten- to twenty-story structures appears on the southeastern side of the airport. The air force's hangars and parking area flash by on the left, as the modern airport terminal appears on the right; beyond lies the general aviation and repair shacks, and in the misty distance the high volcano mountain range appears.

Whether arriving by air or land (few come by ship these days), the arrival to Guatemala can be a memorable experience. For all the attention focused on Central America, this is a country still shrouded in confusing mystery for most North Americans. This book was therefore inspired by a desire to explore, for an American audience, this environment—this complex puzzle.

In sifting through its recent experience, one begins to uncover Guatemala's vulnerable form of development. On an episodic basis, events have received considerable attention. This attention, as well as the intricate character of the society, has not made for an easy analytical task. The ascendancy of a very fragile democracy in 1986 operates not only in a national but also a regional political development framework, thus adding other levels of analysis. The United States' involvement and interest in these matters provide yet another layer of perspectives.

In the present assessment, the two authors attempt a chronicle of Guatemala's modern political development as a prelude to an analysis of the nation's current environment. That is an ambitious task, given the self-imposed manuscript length. To be sure, this is not written in an attempt to be encyclopedic in tone and character. Much about Guatemala's rich history and complex society is left out for the sake of space and coherent analysis. And to some degree this streamlined review puts forth the authors' own judgments about events and trends. Yet, with *Guatemala's Political Puzzle* we hope to have provided a credible rendering of the situation of a nation that ultimately is, and will remain, an anchor to Central American developments.

This book is not the product of a traditional research exercise. Although both authors have traveled widely in Guatemala, this is an analytical piece designed to provide a fresh interpretation to some well known (and some less well known) and, at times, distorted facts. In completing this work, the secondary literature was reviewed as a supplement to the authors' own in-country assessments. A review of some of that literature, and sources utilized for background information in this book, is presented at the end of the volume.

The authors have received considerable assistance in preparing this volume, from both the public and private sectors in Guatemala and the United States; and for their help, we thank them. Among them, political figures of various Guatemalan governments, journalists, academics from both Guatemala and the United States, military officers, private sector representatives, the Fundacion para el Desarrollo de Guatemala, and others in private life have provided much assistance. Several current and former officials of the American government's executive and legislative branches provided useful comments and timely assistance. Naturally, any errors or misjudgments to be found in this volume are the authors' own.

Washington, D.C.
Summer 1987

Guatemala in Tables

Table 1
National Executives of Guatemala: 1838–1987

Character of Governance	National Executive	Years in Office	Form of Succession
Conservative	Rivera Paz	1838–39	Overthrown
Liberal	General Salazar	January–April 1839	Overthrown
Conservative	Rivera Paz	1839–44	Phased out
Conservative	Jose Rafael Carrera	1844–48	Resignation
Conservative	Mariano Paredes	1849–51	Overthrown
Conservative	Jose Rafael Carrera	1851–65	Died in bed
Conservative	Gen. Vincente Cerna	1865–71	Overthrown
Liberal	Miguel Garcia Granados	1871–83	Forced resignation
Republican dictatorship	Justo Ruffino Barrios	1873–85	Killed in battle
Republican dictatorship	Manuel Lisandro Barrillas	1885–92	Served extended constitutional term of office
Republican dictatorship	Jose-Maria Reina Barrios	1892–98	Assassinated
Republican dictatorship	Manuel Estrada Cabrera	1898–1920	Overthrown
Unionist	Carlos Herrera	1920	Overthrown
Republican dictatorship	Gen. Jose Maria Orellana	1921–26	Died of heart attack
Republican dictatorship	Gen. Lazaro Chacon	1926–30	Died of illness
Provisional	Baudilio Palma	12 December–16 December 1930	Overthrown
Provisional	Gen. Manuel Orellana	31 December 1930	Resigned
Provisional	Jose Maria Reina Andrade	31 December 1930–14 February 1931	Resigned
Republican dictatorship	Gen. Jorge Ubico y Castenada	1931–1944	Resigned
Provisional junta	Gen. Federico Ponce Vaides	1 July–20 October 1944	Overthrown

Provisional triumvirate	Major Francisco Arana Captain Jacobo Arbenz Jorge Toriello Garrido	20 October 1944– 14 March 1945	Concluded term with elections
Reformist	Juan Jose Arevalo Bermejo	1945–50	Served electoral term of office
Left-wing Reformist	Col. Jacobo Arbenz	15 March 1950– June 1954	Overthrown
Military junta	Cols. Elfego Mozon and Castillo Armas	27 June– 29 June 1954	Phased out
Conservative	Col. Carlos Castillo Armas	8 July 1954– July 1957	Assassinated
Provisional	Luis Arturo Gonzalez Lopez	July–October 1957	Resigned
Provisional	Guillermo Flores Avendano	October 1957– 2 March 1958	Concluded term with elections
Archaic Republican dictatorship	Gen. Miguel Ydigoras Fuentes	1958–63	Overthrown
Military Constitutional Reformist	Col. Enrique Peralta Azurdia	1963–65	Concluded term with elections
Protected Democracy	Julio Cesar Mendez Montenegro	1966–70	Served electoral term of office
Repressive Republicanism	Col. Carlos Arana Osorio	1970–74	Served electoral term of office
Repressive Republicanism	Gen. Eugenio Kjell Laugerud Garcia	1974–78	Served electoral term of office
Repressive Republicanism	Gen. Romeo Lucas Garcia	1978–82	Overthrown
Military Constitutional Reformist	Military junta (triumvirate)	March 1982– June 1982	Phased out
Military Constitutional Reformist	Gen. Efrain Rios Montt	June 1982– August 1983	Palace coup
Military Constitutional Reformist	Gen. Oscar Humberto Mejia Victores	August 1983– January 1986	Concluded term with elections
Nascent Democratic	Marco Vinicio Cerezo Arevalo	January 1986–	

Table 2
Socioeconomic Data

Land Area:	42,042 square miles
Religion:	Roman Catholic, traditional
Language:	Spanish, many Indian languages
Literacy:	50 percent
Life Expectancy:	60 years (national average)
Economy:	
Industries:	food processing cement textiles mining
Export Crops:	coffee cotton sugar bananas meat

SOURCE: *National Geographic Magazine,* National Geographic Society, 1986.

Table 3
Key Economic Indicators[1]

	1985	Projected 1986
Domestic Economy		
Population (millions)	8.0	8.2
Population growth (%)	3.0	3.0
Gross Domestic Product (in current dollars)	8,900.0	9,200.0
Per Capita GDP (in current dollars)	1,110.0	1,100.0
GDP in local currency (1985 quetzals)	2,925.0	2,925.0
Consumer Price Index (% change)	18.7	35.0
Production and Employment		
Labor Force (1,000s)	2,500.0	2,600.0
Reported Unemployment (average % for year)	13.0	14.0
Industrial production (% change)	− 1.3	-0-
Fiscal deficit as % of GDP	− 0.8	− 2.5
Balance of Payments		
Balance on current account	− 246.0	− 38.0
Commercial balance	− 17.0	153.0
Exports	1,060.0	1,119.0
Imports	1,077.0	966.0
Services	− 248.0	− 239.0
Transfers	20.0	49.0
Balance on capital account	329.0	36.0
Private	243.0	136.0
Long term	61.0	53.0
Short term	182.0	83.0
Official and Bank	86.0	− 101.0
Long term	61.0	29.0
Short term	25.0	− 130.0
Errors and Omissions	− 14.0	—
Total reserve variation	− 69.0	2.0

Exports of Goods

Total	1,060.0	1,119.0
Central American Common Market	208.0	200.0
Rest of world	852.0	919.0
Traditional	652.0	666.0
Coffee	451.0	493.0
Cotton	73.0	35.0
Bananas	71.0	76.0
Meat	10.0	3.0
Sugar	46.0	59.0
Non-traditional	200.0	253.0
Cardamom	61.0	60.0
Petroleum	12.0	28.0
Other	127.0	165.0

[1]In millions of U.S. dollars, unless otherwise noted.

SOURCES: Bank of Guatemala Reports and American Embassy estimates, as cited in *Foreign Economic Trends and Their Implications for the United States: Guatemala,* prepared by the American Embassy Guatemala for the U.S. Department of Commerce, International Trade Administration (September 1986), and *Guatemala 1986: The Year of Promises,* Inforpress Centroamericana, p. 31 (January 1987), which bases its figures from its own sources, as well as both ECLAC and Bank of Guatemala figures.

Table 4
U.S.–Guatemalan Relations:
Trade and Foreign Assistance Levels[1]

	Economic Assistance			
Year	ESF (Economic Support Funds)	DA (Development Assistance)	PL 480 (Public Law 480)	Total
1980	0.0	7.8	3.3	11.1
1981	0.0	9.1	7.5	16.6
1982	0.0	8.2	5.6	13.8
1983	10.0	12.2	5.3	27.5
1984	0.0	4.4	11.6	16.0
1984[2]	0.0	16.6	0.0	16.6
1985	12.5	40.1	20.4	73.0
1986	47.9	36.9	20.9	111.0
1987	58.6	33.3	23.4	143.6

	Military Assistance			
Year	MAP (Military Assistance Program)	FMS (Foreign Military Sales)	IMET (International Military Education and Training)	Total
1980	0.0	0.0	0.0	0.0
1981	0.0	0.0	0.0	0.0
1982	0.0	0.0	0.0	0.0
1983	0.0	0.0	0.0	0.0
1984	0.0	0.0	0.0	0.0
1984[2]	0.0	0.0	0.0	0.0
1985	0.0	0.0	0.3	0.3
1986	5.0	0.0	0.356	5.356
1987	5.0	0.0	0.4	5.4

Guatemalan–U.S. Trade

Year	Guatemalan Exports to U.S.	Guatemalan Imports from U.S.
1980	419.9	551.8
1981	223.3	565.9
1982	306.0	432.3
1983	405.1	365.3
1984	435.5	414.2
1985	407.0	445.1
1986 (projected)	435.0	395.0

[1]In millions of U.S. dollars, unless otherwise noted.
[2]Supplemental allocation for year indicated.

SOURCES: *Sustaining a Consistent Policy in Latin America: One Year After the National Bipartisan Commission Report,* Special Report #124, U.S. Department of State, April 1985; Bank of Guatemala Reports and American Embassy estimates, as cited in *Foreign Economic Trends and Their Implications for the United States: Guatemala,* prepared by the American Embassy Guatemala for the U.S. Department of Commerce, International Trade Administration (September 1986); *Direction of Trade Statistics: Yearbook 1986,* International Monetary Fund, Washington, D.C., 1986; and additional information supplied by Guatemala Desk, U.S. Department of State.

Table 5
Guerrilla Group Development
and Revolutionary Organizations

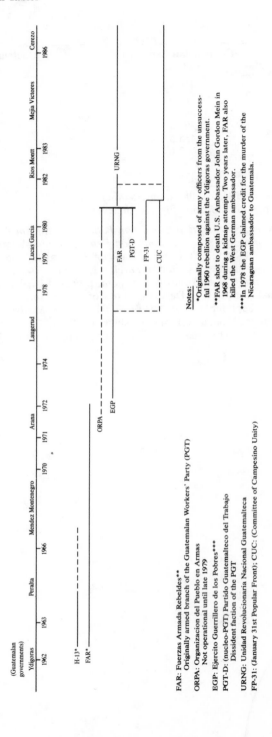

FAR: Fuerzas Armada Rebeldes**
    Originally armed branch of the Guatemalan Workers' Party (PGT)

ORPA: Organizacion del Pueblo en Armas
    Not operational until late 1979

EGP: Ejercito Guerrillero de los Pobres***

PGT-D: (nucleo-PGT) Partido Guatemalteco del Trabajo
    Dissident faction of the PGT

URNG: Unidad Revolucionaria Nacional Guatemalteca

FP-31: (January 31st Popular Front); CUC: (Committee of Campesino Unity)

Notes:

*Originally composed of army officers from the unsuccess-
ful 1960 rebellion against the Ydigoras government.

**FAR shot to death U.S. Ambassador John Gordon Mein in
1968 during a kidnap attempt. Two years later, FAR also
killed the West German ambassador.

***In 1978 the EGP claimed credit for the murder of the
Nicaraguan ambassador to Guatemala.

Table 6
Guatemala's 1985 Presidential Elections:
Results of First and Second Rounds

Candidate/Party	First Round % Votes[1]	Second Round % Votes[2]
VINICIO CEREZO Christian Democratic (DCG)	38.59	69.52
JORGE CARPIO-NICOLLE Union of the National Center (UCN)	20.28	31.48
JORGE SERRANO ELIAS Democratic Party of National Reconciliation (PDCN)	13.80	—
MARIO SANDOVAL ALARCON National Liberation Movement (MLN-PID)	12.52	—
MARIO DAVID GARCIA Nationalistic Authentic Central (CAN)	6.29	—
MARIO SOLORZANO Social Democratic Party (PSD)	3.42	—
ALEJANDRO MALDONADO AGUIRRE National Renewal Party (PNR)	3.15	—
LEONEL SISNIEGA-OTERO Anti-Communist Unification Party (PUA-MEC-FUN)	1.90	—

[1]99.95% of votes tabulated.
[2]98% of votes tabulated.

SOURCES: Supreme Electoral Tribunal, Guatemala; and U.S. Department of State.

Table 7
Guatemala's Contemporary Political Landscape

CAN:
:   Central Autentica Nacionalista
    Conservative political party formed in 1974.

DCG:
:   Democracia Cristiana Guatemalteca
    The Christian Democratic Party of Guatemala, which won the 1985 elections.

EGP:
:   Ejercito Guerrillero de los Pobres
    Marxist guerrilla group founded in 1972; member of URNG command.

FAR:
:   Frente Armadas Rebeldes
    Marxist guerrilla group originally founded in 1962; member of URNG command.

FUN:
:   Frente de Unidad Nacional
    Right-wing political party formed in 1977.

FUR:
:   Frente Unido de la Revolucion
    Left/social democratic group founded in 1977.

GAM:
:   Grupo de Apoyo Mutuo para Familiares de Desparecidos
    Human rights group formed in 1984.

La Mano Blanca, Ojo por Ojo, Ejercito Secreto Anticomunista, and Escuadron de la Muerte: Right-wing extremist groups of the 1970s and early 1980s.

MEC:
:   Movimiento Emergente de Concordia
    Right-wing political party founded in the mid-1980s by supporters of Colonel Francisco Gordillo Martinez, a member of the initial three-man junta following the March 1982 coup.

MDN:
:   Movimiento Democratico Nacional
    Right-wing political party formed by Castillo Armas following the 1954 revolution. Dissident members of the party shortly after its inception broke ranks and formed the MLN.

MLN:
:   Movimiento de Liberacion Nacional
    Righ-wing political party of conservative standard-bearer Mario Sandoval Alarcon, dating back to the late 1950s.

MR-13:
:   Movimiento Revolucionario 13 de Noviembre
    Trotskyist guerrilla group formed in the mid-1960s by Colonel Marco Antonio Yon Sosa and comprised of dissident army officers.

ORPA:
:   Organizacion Revolucionaria del Pueblo en Armas
    Marxist guerrilla group founded in 1979; member of the URNG command.

PAR:
:   Partido de Accion Revolucionario
    Reformist political party organized by Juan Jose Arevalo in the early 1940s; superseded by an amalgamation of factions during the 1950 elections of Colonel Jacobo Arbenz.

PDCN/MAS: Partido Democratico de Cooperacion Nacional
Moderate conservative political party organized in 1984. After the 1985 elections, elements of the party defected and formed the Movimiento de Accion Solidaria (MAS).

PGT: Partido Guatemalteco del Trabajo
Founded in 1949 as originally the Communist party of Guatemala, in the 1980s, it has been tied to the URNG.

PID: Partido Institucional Democratico
Right-wing political party formed in 1965.

PNR: Partido Nacionalista Renovador
Moderate conservative political party formed in the late 1970s.

PR: Partido Revolucionario
Moderate reformist political party, with a strong following in the 1960s and early 1970s.

PSD: Partido Socialista Democratico
Social Democratic party, returned from exile in 1985.

PUA: Partido de Unificacion Anticomunista
Small, very conservative off-shoot of the MLN.

URNG: Unidad Revolucionaria Nacional Guatemalteca
Unified command of the major guerrilla groups, formed in 1982.

UCN: Union del Centro Nacional
Centrist political party founded in 1983, and runner-up in the 1985 presidential elections.

1
Setting the Stage: The Political Puzzle

The Democratic Challenge

Guatemala's break with authoritarianism in late 1985 involved a process with some dramatic moments. It is too early to tell whether this break is substantial, although clearly the successful transfer of power from military rule to a civilian and democratically elected government was unto itself meaningful. The process toward the January 1986 inauguration of Vinicio Cerezo survived the onslaught of the left-wing and the right-wing forces, as well as civilian and military pressures. Thus, the appropriate question to be asked is: How solid and legitimate is the new political environment?

The transfer of power in early 1986 was preceded by generally proper elections in 1984 (of a Constituent Assembly) and in 1985 of the incoming civilian government. This made it possible, in theory, to begin differentiating between the public's perhaps reluctant acceptance of the governing incumbents—a military government—and genuine understanding of, and commitment to, a new and democratic political system. If only measured by the electoral turnout in late 1985 and the relative order that ultimately surrounded the entire process, Guatemalans clearly voted for change. Some voted for change and reforms, while many probably simply voted for peace and stability—all of which have been in short supply in Guatemala in recent years.

The events of 1985 were not a referendum on the military regime; for almost the first time in the nation's history, this institution was not a direct party in this contest, which involved only civilian politicians bidding for the top prize. But the military regimes of Rios Montt and Mejia Victores did establish the rules and ensuing pace of progress toward a political opening. To their credit, while the armed forces fiddled with the process, in the final analysis they did not abort it. Thus, while the military set the broader framework of rules, the civilians played the narrow electoral game. As of January 1986, these civilians have managed the broader political game and even have the institutional mechanisms to modify the rules.

Who, then, has the capability to influence the destinies of Guatemala's newly found political springtime? Although foreign actors, ranging

1

from the U.S. Congress to forces in Havana, and those within the international economic community and attendant environment will have a continuing impact, the fundamental responsibilities lie among Guatemala's political elites. These elites now have to assure not only the functioning of the system but also its sustenance with results and popular support. The 1984–85 electoral sequence merely provided a vital mechanism for demonstrating and asserting legitimacy; the durability of the regime is another matter.

At this juncture there is certainly, at minimum, a recognition of the propriety of the new government; in a static sense, such recognition affords President Vinicio Cerezo the aura of legitimacy. This is a very important, if amorphous, measure of the recent change in the Guatemalan quality of governance. But while the 1985 elections generated a degree of credibility among the international community for the nation's democratic process, this must be distinguished from the depth of trust the Christian Democratic government will be able to generate for itself among the citizenry at large through the next scheduled elections.

The projected 1990 elections will provide clarification of the basic legitimacy of this Guatemalan political experiment. At that juncture, the projected succession of administrations within a democratic framework will begin to generate an important distinction: support for the nation's political aspirants as opposed to genuine commitment to the government's democratic character. In other words, the projected 1990 elections will provide some empirical measure of the depth of the institutionalization of democratic practice in Guatemalan society.

One challenge to Guatemala's popularly elected government is whether a practical distinction between military authoritarianism and civilian democratic rule will hold up in the perceptions of Guatemalans when it comes to visible results. Will the nation's economic difficulties be resolved to the point of generating employment and attendant increased standards of living? Will the insurgency be permanently eliminated? Will common criminal activity abate?

The dismal state of the nation in recent years would suggest that the regimes associated with the previous era are totally discredited, and therefore not an attractive alternative. The successful 1985 electoral exercise provides clear societal support of this hypothesis. But elections and regime support are two distinct factors. When it came to voting, the violent authoritarianism of the late 1970s and early 1980s probably elicited stronger negative passions than generated deep support for the democratic system presently in place. While unclear as to the intended direction of civilian rule, it is likely that the only thing

Guatemalans knew for sure was that something had to change. For the nation's new democratic leadership, the political challenge has therefore become the degree to which it is capable of evoking broadly based loyalties for the regime. In this context, rhetoric will not do; concrete results are required.

After the euphoria of the early weeks of the transition in 1986, segments of the citizenry quickly settled back into their proverbial cynicism about government. Old or new, this was now just "the government." Such an attitude was hardly surprising in light of the shallow margin of national consensus the incoming government had on sociopolitical issues. The slow-moving economic program of the new government, as well as the highly visible if uncertain diplomatic maneuvers in Central America by the president of Guatemala, would suggest evolutionary dynamics rather than major changes. While it would perhaps be easy to condemn the Cerezo government on this issue alone, at this juncture one should be appreciative of the difficult agenda it needs to pursue in order to maintain itself, let alone succeed. It is more than likely that the new administration was surprised at its own successful conquest of the National Palace, leading to some initial confusion and caution in governance.

To instill legitimacy, measured through credibility and trust, Guatemalan democracy faces the unenviable mission of having to shift natural dynamics from strictly political to broader social standards. The historical monopoly of stark and simplistic ideological values will have to blend in with some degree of societal consciousness; this will be a sign of the modernization of Guatemalan society. Over the next several years, this suggests a change in priorities by the nation's political and economic elites from formal and narrow political democracy to "social" democracy—the latter a term with much-abused connotations in the Central American context. But such a task will not be simple, as it implies a new consensus of values across the nation's philosophically divided political spectrum.

Participatory democracy and the rights of individuals to express themselves bear also on attitudes toward private property and economic management of society. Any modification of the social landscape is likely to entail bitter debate over economic philosophies, a salient concern in a society where the compilation of nineteenth century liberalism and modern-day market economics has youthful and articulate proponents. There remains the distinct possibility that the system may overreach itself beyond what a conservative (and therefore cautious) society is capable of absorbing if pushed by severe internal and external pressures.

While critics have tended to exaggerate the issue, the government will continue to operate with a variable lack of practical autonomy from conservative elite and military constituencies. To a degree, Vinicio Cerezo will remain encumbered by policies pursued by guerrilla forces and other left-wing groups. Thus, while the administration's margin of maneuverability will be somewhat circumscribed, this does not suggest that a democratic government in Guatemala is beholden to a narrow cluster of special interests. While this underlines the relatively high degree of polarization within Guatemalan society, limits on executive branch authority are nevertheless characteristic of republican governance. In this search for a democratic order, the overarching goal will be to bring diverse constituencies into a coherent political community; in fact, this continued search for pluralism is the key to encouraging a maturation of Guatemala's fledgling democracy.

Keys to the Guatemalan Puzzle

Guatemala has historically emerged only occasionally and for brief moments above the horizon of the international news media. When it has done so, the projected image of this Central American nation has been less than favorable. Any attempt to provide a legitimate evaluation of Guatemala's tentative return to democratic rule must therefore be viewed in the context of its political experience and traditions. It is the legacy of the nation's difficult socioeconomic and political development that has shaped the character of the regime transition. What is distinctive about this legacy?

Preceding Guatemala's development in the colonial period through the early nineteenth century are the cultural roots of a strong Mayan heritage. Surviving even the most turbulent periods in history, this indigenous heritage has provided a singular basis to the national character. It has also generated a challenge to the formation of modern Guatemala. Historically, the indigenous population has been removed from national development. But flowing from the nation's transition to modernizing political rule in this century, there has been a growing appreciation of the necessity to promote socioeconomic and political development on a truly national basis. How to blend the nation's heritage into this process has been a challenge. Thus, the manner in which the past is to be integrated with the future is the political and developmental puzzle of the nation.

Since the end of the colonial era, Guatemala's march of history has occurred in a traditional environment. This has been marked by small doses of institutional development, with the Catholic church and the armed forces constituting the early cast of characters. Not surprisingly, without an adequately matured civilian political sector, the country has been governed by the military—at first, men on horseback and, more recently, army commands. Government changeovers have occurred by military impetus. Flowing from this unsatisfactory framework, the character of Guatemalan governance has ranged from traditional authoritarian rule by caudillos, to social revolutionary movements, to direct military rule, and, most recently, to transition to democratic government.

Several salient characteristics have marked all governmental experiments. First, while the modern conception of the role of the military in Latin America has been that of an institution that has eclipsed periods of civilian rule, in Guatemala the armed forces have in fact provided, and embodied, the only real models of governance. Second, reflecting the impact of the nation's distinct cultural heritage, which at times has bordered on outright chauvinism, all of Guatemala's political movements have been marked by a strong vein of nationalistic fervor. Third, an inability to seek out moderate styles of governance has from time to time led the nation toward extremist models of both a highly conservative or liberal character. This has particularly been the case in the post–World War II period. Finally, reflecting Guatemala's turbulent development, the nation's political experiences have generally been abruptly terminated by the action of the final arbiter of society—military authority.

Guatemalans are ultimately the key element in the trials and tribulations of their own society. It is a bit disingenuous to attempt to transfer explanations for the nation's difficult development experience to external actors. Arguing for "dependency theory" and the purported nefarious role of the industrialized world, or reaching back to the antiquity of times for social explanations, are poor devices to avoid an effective critique of modern Guatemalan political culture. Obviously, Guatemala has not been immune from the ravages of the colonial era, nor is the nation's turbulent sociopolitical experience solely the result of an inborn societal feature. Instead, the Guatemalan record derives from the above, and more. The character of this historical experience is exemplified by the manner in which basic cultural values and attitudes have been transmitted over the last 150 years.

What is it that has been transmitted? The primary model of governance has been authoritarian in character, exploitative in style, and military in institutional terms. This has over the long term reflected the hierarchical and paternalistic character of sociopolitical life. Political modernization has occurred through constitutional trappings generally viewed as abstract legal necessities, rather than guidelines of political behavior. As the prevalent model of government, authoritarian and personalistic regimes have acted as both predator of political development and agents of change.

Alternative forms of political regimes—liberal (in the nineteenth-century sense of the term), civilian, and reformist—have rarely been given much of a chance. When there have been shifts, the polity has swung widely between political extremes. Much of the reformist and civilian variant in governance has in fact been short-lived, inclined toward experimentations, and prone to violent countermovements. The relative absence of moderation in the Guatemalan political scene has tended to limit the range of official ideology and curtail public mobilization. When the latter has occurred (on and off by the left, since the 1950s), it has done so in a vacuum of modernized political mechanisms and institutions. Not surprisingly, until the 1985 elections, for example, Guatemala cannot be said to have had a viable panoply of political party structures and relationships. In the context of the nation's twentieth-century development experience, alternatives to the primary model of governance have therefore been generally equated with radicalism.

This suggests that Guatemala has suffered from an inability to resolve a major dilemma: Is the function of government to promote political and socioeconomic development, or is its mission to stave off major change and sustain the status quo? In answering this basic question, the military, as the nation's premier institution, has demonstrated considerable institutional resolution, but has embraced a variety of political models. Contrary to the popular image, not all Guatemalan officers think alike and hold the same degree of social consciousness. A glance at Table 1 in this volume reveals the variance in the character of military governance from left-wing reformism to conservative repression. What is also often forgotten is that the early waves of insurgencies in the 1960s were in fact the products of disgruntled, mid-level military officers.

Guatemala has attracted a certain level of international attention as a result of the very nature of these leftist and rightist currents. The reformist character of the 1944 revolution degenerated into a quasi-communist regime by the early 1950s—from which ensued American intervention in 1954. This experiment was replaced by a succession of initially archaic but progressively modernizing regimes searching for a new political order. That experience ultimately degenerated into near chaos in the early 1980s—from which has ensued the democratic elections of 1985.

Critical at each turning point have been the armed forces and segments of the political elite. While the civilian political classes have since the 1950s developed constituencies and power bases of their own, the army has provided the distinctive human and political component in the nation's search for governance. In an ironic development, it was also a military government that oversaw the democratic elections of 1985.

That Guatemala, let alone its armed forces, has come out of these succeeding political crises in one piece—if not intact—is quite extraordinary. Clearly, scars do run deep and the human losses are profound and tragic. For the army, the experience has been traumatic; for the Guatemalan people, the experience of the last forty years remains indecisive. On a regional scale of political development, where Central America fares badly, Guatemala has had a generally more acute political process. Its extremist tendencies have swung the farthest and its tenacious and violent character has, as a result, received extensive and long-running international attention. What is significant is that the system inched itself back toward moderation after 1984 and a semblance of democratic government by January 1986, while neighboring El Salvador and Nicaragua have remained in an open state of turmoil. Obviously, this complicated story is still unfolding.

2
Understanding Guatemala: Foundations of the Society

Introduction

Guatemala has a beautiful geographical and cultural landscape, and a controversial polity. Any nation with such characteristics is bound to engender deep interest and profound emotions. And why not? To a degree, Guatemala's soul lies in its extraordinary geography. Here is a country that includes Lake Atitlan, located 5,000 feet above sea level with an uncomparable series of volcanoes as a backdrop. The natural perspective is so breathtaking that, along with other Guatemalan scenes, it generates a moment of emotion from an otherwise proper and scholarly historian:

> Guatemala's Lake Atitlan . . . is one of the most beautiful on Earth. More remote, but rivalling Atitlan in their misty tranquility, are the tiny highland lakes north of Huehuetenango. Lake Amatitlan, a popular resort . . . combines breathtaking views with warm mineral-water springs. In the tropical lowlands are Lake Izabal, which is connected to the Gulf of Honduras and the Caribbean via the exotic Rio Dulce, and Lake Peten-Itza, in the midst of which lies the island village of Flores. (Near Peten-Itza are the ancient Mayan ruins of Uaxactun and Tikal.) (Woodward, 1985, p. 4–5)

Guatemala has a quality tourism potential simply waiting to be developed. What has held it back? To a great extent, the answer to this question relates to the staggeringly unhappy experience of the country over the past forty years with severe bouts of instability.

In writing this book the authors have a tentatively hopeful story to tell about a fundamentally fascinating country. In part, it is a remarkable country because of the juxtaposing of inherent natural beauty and quaintness with a harsh political and economic reality. Guatemala is not a wealthy country, but its people are gifted. Guatemala's image has been tarnished by recent periods of violence, but its immediate future is laced with encouraging opportunities. Guatemala's civilian leadership has not demonstrated a complete maturation, yet events in

9

1985 and 1986 began to suggest that the damning label the country had acquired in the recent past could be due for a change. And while Guatemala is a potential paradise, like the rest of the countries of the world, it is neither Eden nor hell.

The Nation in Review

Of the five nations of Central America (Costa Rica, El Salvador, Guatemala, Honduras, Nicaragua), Guatemala has both the largest population, with 8 million inhabitants, and the largest economy, with an estimated gross domestic product (GDP) in 1986 of $9,200 million. With a total area of 42,042 square miles (about the size of Tennessee), it is smaller than both Honduras and Nicaragua. Roughly 80 percent of the population, including inhabitants of Guatemala City, lives in the highland region that extends from the Mexican border southeast toward the Salvadoran and Honduran borders. This area is relatively temperate in climate, with a rich, productive soil, but rugged in geography. In contrast, tropical weather and attendant traditional export crop operations (cotton, coffee, and sugar) dominate the Pacific coastal lowlands. Neither the Caribbean region nor the immense tropical jungle of the Peten northeastern sector represent large populations or areas of economic activity.

In proportions unmatched elsewhere in Central America, on an ethnic level Guatemala is an Indian country. The descendants of the Mayas contribute an estimated 55 percent of the total population, living primarily in the central highlands and outward toward the Mexican border. To a remarkable degree, Guatemala's Indians have retained their indigenous customs and language. In fact, Spanish is often not the dominant language and one is likely to encounter portions of the population that do not speak Spanish at all. The highlands (Altiplano) have, until very recently, constituted a fairly isolated Indian society, participating only marginally in the nation's urban political and economic life. Communication, economic growth, and political developments in this region have since the 1940s begun to affect this traditional identity.

Obviously, Guatemala is also very much a Hispanicized or Europeanized society, and thus one of mixed ethnic and cultural descent. Roughly 40 percent or more of the population is described as *ladino,* a hard-to-define category that highlights more the degree of cultural and social assimilation than actual ethnicity. Aside from the original Spanish stock, immigration to Guatemala during the nineteenth century brought small clusters of various groups including: Germans (who developed coffee cultivation); Belgians; Christian Lebanese; Jews from Central Europe; Chinese; an almost negligible Black population; and, in the twentieth century, a small colony of Americans.

Guatemala is a youthful and growing country. Its population of 8 million has an annual average rate of growth of roughly 2.9 percent (one of the highest rates in Latin America), and approximately 55 percent of Guatemalans are under the age of 15. The nation has been increasingly urbanized (as opposed to "urban")—reaching the 40 percent mark in present times—in contrast to about 15 percent some twenty-five years ago. The resultant pressures of these changes on both the social and economic environment are considerable. For example, the adult literacy rate is only 55 percent, but is significantly lower in rural areas, at approximately 20 percent. Rural sanitation remains poor and urban services are overtaxed; the same is true of health care and education. Life expectancy has been measured at approximately 57 to 61 years (male/female) but is dramatically lower for the Indian population (44 years). Rural infant malnutrition is a serious problem, and infant mortality is high (about 78–80 per 1,000 live births). As in other parts of the Third World, housing is inadequate and represents an increasing challenge in urbanized areas, where a population fleeing from rural areas has created shantytowns surrounding Guatemala City proper.

These stark living conditions were made comparatively more difficult over the last decade by a combination of three factors. First, the oil price shocks in the mid-1970s led to a relocation of export earnings to convert energy imports, which subsequently forced substantial increases in the traditionally low level of inflation in Guatemala. Second, the earthquake of February 1976 ripped through much of the highland region (including the capital), killing some 30,000 people and leaving an estimated 20 percent of the population temporarily homeless. This tragedy forced the government to reassess its budget priorities. Third, beginning in the mid-1970s and growing dramatically through the early 1980s, the nation underwent a brutal rural insurgency, with urban terrorism and a random crime wave. As a result, the foreign investment and tourist sectors fled the nation and further generated a bleeding of national resources through capital flight.

Despite the challenges, the Guatemalan economy survived and, in certain circumstances, actually made dramatic comebacks. The oil crisis of the mid-1970s was cushioned by a growth in tourism, high coffee prices, and the nation's then-substantial foreign exchange reserves, which reached a peak in 1978 (over 700 million quetzals). The aftermath of the 1976 earthquake actually produced a small economic boom through a short-term inflow of foreign assistance and increased public investment programs. Investments in Guatemala's nascent oil exploration operations brought additional inflows of capital.

This enviable record was negatively affected by a series of developments in the late 1970s from which Guatemala is only now beginning to extricate itself. On the economic side, the Lucas Garcia government (1978–82) engaged in a number of costly and ultimately inefficient public investment projects (for example, communications, hydroelectricity, timber, paper plants) just prior to a steep decline in government revenues. The situation was made worse by external political developments. The 1979 revolution in Nicaragua and the governmental breakdown in El Salvador destabilized Guatemala's lucrative Central American trade, a development from which the country has yet to recover. And finally, by 1980, the political risk impact on business activity attributed to domestic violence threw the economy into crisis. However, Guatemala's economic hemorrhage was slowed down by the subsequent Rios Montt and Mejia Victores regimes (1982–85) through the institution of severe fiscal austerity policies. Thus, the early 1980s witnessed a period of recession, but it was also marked by an increasing involvement of the government in the national economy.

Since 1982, hopes have hinged on the positive impact a renewed democratic and stabilized political situation would have on the economy. While the long-term economic verdict is still out, the six-year decline of the economy appears to have been curbed, perhaps less by conscious government action than by psychology and simple luck. There is no doubt that confidence levels, from tourists to investors, have been positively impacted by visions of renewed societal stability and productivity. Although coffee revenues have been unpredictable due to changing international market prices, the larger volume of nontraditional exports (for example, fruits and flowers) encouraged by the U.S. Caribbean Basin Initiative (CBI) have been positive economic developments. Tourism has rebounded, and the nation's democratic image has borne fruits in the form of assistance and credit packages from the United States, West Germany, France, and Italy. On the domestic front, pent-up demand has stimulated growth in the construction sector, while public investments in social infrastructure have suggested further economic activity.

On the other hand, other traditional sectors (sugar, in particular) have not witnessed positive effects from either Guatemala's new democracy or favorable international trends. The continued dependence on foreign exchange earned through the export of key agricultural products (cotton, coffee, sugar) and the vagaries of international pricing will continue to play havoc on the national economic picture. Fortunately, Guatemala's diversified climate permits an expansion into a variety of food crops, permitting a self-sufficiency in basic commodities (corn, rice, beans) and an increasing surplus for exports in alternative products.

The nation's natural resource potential (oil, hydroelectricity, timber, and fisheries, in particular) has encountered difficulties in development, although still provides considerable possibilities. The energy sector has received the most attention, since amounts of low-quality crude oil have been discovered in both the northern and Peten regions of the country. In this context, a small extraction capability by pipeline has been developed. Exploration continues and awaits encouragement, among other factors, relating to government hydrocarbon laws and regulations as well as the protection of installations against guerrilla attacks.

A core tenet of the new democratic government's platform has been a pledge for a more equal distribution of the benefits of development. It is too early to tell how this will be accomplished and whether government actions will have the desired effect. Previous Guatemalan governments have generally pursued liberal, free trade policies; foreign investment has been welcomed, although bureaucratic red tape has tried the regime. While governmental interference has traditionally been kept to a minimum (by regional standards), by the 1970s the nation fell victim to the development of a series of inefficient parastatal institutions (particularly under the Arana government, 1970–74). Still, a relatively low public sector investments policy has afforded Guatemala an enviably low public external debt (U.S. $2.5 billion estimated in 1986). Aside from new borrowing, rescheduling, and foreign credits, the Cerezo administration has proposed to generate national resources by increasing the government's fiscal revenues. This is likely to be a difficult campaign as the private sector will, with some legitimacy, resist higher taxation in the early stages of economic recovery. However, disappointing tax collections have been as much an economic as a sociopolitical challenge in Guatemala; profound philosophical differences over citizens' social responsibilities and economic fairness have kept a resolution of this question consistently out of reach.

The Pillars of Society

Central America's primary societal institutions, including those of Guatemala, are changing. Until recently, Guatemala had a relatively stable oligarchy, although it had been maintained through the use of coercion and electoral fraud. Government, private forces, and insurgents had used violence against opponents to ensure the continuity or downfall of regimes, if not society. Thus, years of fratricidal violence led to a sharp polarization of public life.

The balance between civilian leadership and the armed forces has always been at the heart of the political equation in Guatemala; with the election of Vinicio Cerezo as representative of the initiative toward democratic civilian rule, a new calculus to this equation is being forged. The actual value assigned to this new definition of the nation's polity remains dependent upon an assessment of which institutions hold the reins of power in contemporary Guatemalan society. In this context, there can be no doubt that the military remains a major force today. Furthermore, it is clear that its historical involvement has been both profound and, in varying ways, malignant.

It would be simplistic to view the military as the "bad guys" and civilian political actors as the "good guys." In some respects the armed forces have also proven to be a modernizing force within Guatemala, recently anxious to gain support through extensive rural development/civic action programs and by presiding over the management of the return to democratic government. Naturally, with the latter, civilian authority has acquired a new and potential preponderance it had not previously experienced over the army. Yet, the most matured and therefore powerful institutional force in the country remains the armed forces command. In the residual political space, the private sector, and to a lesser degree, the Catholic church remain influential institutions. In a politically pungent fashion, the nation's successive waves of guerrilla-sponsored violence have represented a potent element, bringing the nation to the brink of disaster. And perhaps the weakest link in this equation has been Guatemala's very large indigenous community.

Guatemala's social landscape is more appropriately evaluated against a backdrop not of poverty but rather of obstacles to structural change; the resolution of this development dilemma remains an obstruction to the maturation of democratic rule. In an historical perspective, cultural factors and authoritarian social traditions have discouraged constructive personal initiative. Furthermore, an insular mentality demonstrated by the elite has also hindered the type of social progress that a greater sense of community consciousness might make possible.

In stark ideological terms, there has been a propensity in governing circles to subordinate the struggle against communism to a broader campaign designed to stifle any form of societal modernization. Prior to 1982, this, for example, led to the almost fatal strategic error of not linking the tactics of a counterinsurgency effort to a political campaign designed to win the hearts and minds of a highland Indian population facing a destructive Marxist insurgency. Such an oversight also nearly culminated in the total alienation of the urbanized middle class. Alleviating the aggravation of social and economic tensions and arresting rapid political polarization have been elements in short supply in Guatemalan society.

At this juncture, let us briefly review some chief players in Guatemala's political equation: (1) the civilian political elite, (2) the business community, (3) the armed forces, (4) the political left, (5) the churches, and (6) the Indian population.

The Civilian Political Elite

The poverty of the nation and its strongly centralized political character have generated a relatively small ladino political elite. Until the 1940s, the nation's political landscape was dominated by two contending factions: liberals and conservatives (in the nineteenth-century definition of the terms). Generally unchanged for decades, it encompassed a dual structure consisting of an urbanized constituency as well as a rural land-owning elite.

The turbulence of the 1940s and the more recent process of modernization added numbers to that elite without altering its politically conservative character. A reformist element took root in the wake of Ubico's downfall in the mid-1940s, which, when their experiments turned sour, created an increasingly military-dominated civilian political structure. Not until the 1984–85 transition period can one witness the resurgence of a decimated civilian political elite, this time with a younger, more modern, moderate character to its political program and makeup. And yet, despite the predominance of military rule between the 1951–85 period, the majority of political parties that remain active today trace their roots back to either the 1944 or 1954 period.

In part, because of the ravages of the 1960s and 1970s, Guatemala's civilian elite of the 1980s is not a deeply intellectual group, although it remains ideologically committed. Somewhat reluctantly, Guatemala's elites have begun accommodating themselves to a form of governance that seeks to respond to other constituencies as well. We will return to this community later in the volume.

The Business Community

The historical overlap between Guatemala's political elite and the nation's economic constituency has made modern Guatemala's business community a crucial actor. At minimum, this sector has given the economic vitality that, despite harsh political conditions, has provided the nation with a basis for current political developments. In historical terms, the weakening of traditional civilian elites in the past two decades and the subsequent narrowing of the political process modified the societal involvement of the business community. This sector became increasingly politicized as tactical allies of the established militarized order and the remaining conservative civilian political leadership. The political image of business suffered with allegations of collusion with the government's violent policies and foreign business interests. Statements by some leaders of the business community during this era only appeared to confirm these reports.

But by the late 1970s, and particularly in the 1980s, the business community began to identify itself more as a private or "nongovernmental" sector, and acquired the quality of a distinct constituency. The rationale behind this evolution was simple: worsening societal and economic conditions distanced this constituency from the governing military leadership. Furthermore, the growing intervention and mismanagement of economic affairs by the military government created dissatisfaction in business circles; portions of the business sector turned into tactical supporters of the democratic process.

A young and socially conscious class of economic elites is now rising to the surface as Guatemala transforms itself from a traditional agrarian society to a nation of a more diversified economy and matured polity. But this change in the urbanized economic elite has not yet replaced the residual influence of Guatemala's powerful agrarian economic elite. The interplay of all these factors has therefore generated a vigorous and powerful business community, with such groups as the Comite Coordinador de Asociaciones Agricolas, Comerciales, Industriales y Financieras (CACIF, founded in 1957) retaining a major voice in economic and, by implication, political affairs.

The Armed Forces

Until events elsewhere in Central America in the mid-1980s pushed it off the front page, the Guatemalan military had attracted the most attention of the region's armed forces. Yet, in light of the nation's regional importance and the central role of the armed forces in national political development, the army command will undoubtedly remain a major actor.

In theory, while the military has been technically apolitical, for about three decades it has increasingly and formally viewed itself as the nation's chief institution. Since the Revolution of 1944, all but two of Guatemala's eleven national executives have been career military officers. This trend has been upheld by the Army Law of 1983 and several predecessors stating that the armed forces' mission as guarantor of the national defense is essentially a coequal, not an adjunct to governmental authority. In effect, the Guatemalan military is a highly autonomous institution, which in recent decades has demonstrated both its strengths and weaknesses. Thus, to insure its structural integrity, it not only has had its own well-defined national mission, but has also managed its own financial institutions, banking facilities, and interests in business ventures.

As a formal military structure, the armed forces have escaped the institutional decay that attacked all other sectors of society. In fact, quite the opposite transpired: By the 1960s, the military began to acquire a broader national mission because the traditional civilian political elites had been weakened. The doctrinaire and ideological character of the mission that ensued polarized Guatemalan society into distinct right- and left-wing tendencies. But by the 1970s, the moderate success of the army's policies against the insurgency generated an additional rationale for control of overall national policy development; this period will be analyzed in detail later in the volume. This "developmentalist" coloration, and the army's difficulties with it, led to an institutional crisis in 1982. The basis of this crisis was a growing fear among younger officers that the armed forces' credibility was severely eroding. But it was the officers corps' residual strength that overcame this institutional crisis, simultaneously staved off a Marxist insurgency campaign, and designed a transition back to civilian rule.

The long-standing professionalization of the Guatemalan officer corps has rested on the establishment of the Escuela Politecnica, founded in 1873. The products of this institution—the junior officer corps—ultimately led the Revolution of 1944. Subsequently, all of Guatemala's major political movements can be traced to their origins in the military, ranging from Col. Arbenz's left-wing adventure in the early 1950s, to the formation of early guerrilla factions in the 1960s as a result of military defections. Thus it is hardly surprising that the armed forces acquired the broader political and economic role noted above.

The contemporary Guatemalan army, as the expression goes, is fairly mean and quite lean. Reforms passed in 1983 have instituted compulsory retirement after thirty years of service, weeding out a top-heavy (general-grade) command structure—rarely the case in the rest of Latin America. This also resulted in a fairly young and dynamic corps, which has demonstrated itself to be increasingly modern if conservative in ideological terms. But there remain overtones of a certain disdain for civilian political culture.

While the Guatemalan army has primarily relied on its own limited resources with regard to supplies, logistics, and training, some foreign influences have played a major role. The United States has been and remains the primary source of aid and equipment even though this bilateral linkage was suspended from the late 1970s through the early 1980s. In a secondary role, Israel has provided assistance in technical areas of counterinsurgency campaigns and as a purveyor of basic military equipment.

The Political Left

The left has had a checkered history in Guatemala. It made its appearance in 1944 in a moderate, nonviolent form, but quickly came under communist influence under Arbenz in 1950. The infiltration of the government apparatus, as well as the labor union movement, essentially dictated its demise in the face of a conservative political establishment. Thus, it was the inability of the civilian political leadership to succeed itself in office with little else but conservative or left-wing variants that ultimately created the standoff, which the armed forces came to dominate.

A militant left came to the surface in the 1960s, and has since been the foundation of a series of brutal insurgency campaigns. Until the present, these campaigns have met with failure, although by 1982 a coalition of guerrilla groups (Unidad Revolucionaria Nacional Guatemalteca—URNG) could claim a significant influence over both territory and population. At the same time it remains unclear to what degree this violent left has ever had a genuine claim on the "hearts and minds" of the population, particularly its rural Indian segment.

A portion of the political left has over the years attempted to test this in the form of organized political party activity. Much of this deteriorated into a bloody battle with the nation's security apparatus and the left ultimately met with disastrous defeat. However, the 1985 elections did bring back a nonviolent social democratic component of the leftist spectrum, with the hope that this might expand further into a left-wing democratic alternative autonomous from the Marxist groups. In light of Guatemalas's conservative political tendencies, such a development will sorely test the depth of Guatemala's political system.

The Churches

The Catholic church is divided along ideological and institutional lines, reflecting the basic distinction now found in the church throughout most of Latin America: a hierarchical establishment, holding onto strict doctrine and the concept of an afterlife; and a so-called popular church, oriented toward the grass-roots level of the population and geared toward an amalgamation of Marxist analytical reasoning and Christian social philosophy.

In Guatemala, the established leadership of the church has not acquired the political character that it has in the last decade in El Salvador or more recently in Nicaragua. In fact, until Cardinal Casariego's death in 1983, archbishops of Guatemala City have been prone to associate themselves with the conservative political order or remain silent on the nation's succession of societal upheavals. By the late 1970s, this created tension within the hierarchy, exemplified by the more progressive bishops attempting to distance themselves from their national superior. Likewise, building on the roots of the 1960s Catholic Action, groups such as the Committee for Justice and Peace and the Committee for Campesino Unity (CUC) were created. This demonstrated the increasing political gap between the established church and a then-broadening left-wing ideological movement, particularly in the Indian communities.

Taking advantage of the church's relative weakness, two religious-based constituencies began to outflank it in political terms. One was the "popular church," which had taken root in great part through the proselytizing of a small group of expatriate priests, lay teachers, and foreign intellectuals. Their sympathies with the political left and guerrilla groups have been openly admitted. Such a connection made them targets of government security policies, with clergymen being killed and foreign priests deported. The degree to which this "liberation theology" church acquired any support from the religious faithful in Guatemala is unclear. In 1984, the crushing of the insurgency and the installation of a new archbishop in Guatemala City, as well as the election in 1985 of a Christian Democratic government have brought together a new agenda for the church's role in Guatemala.

That equation has been complicated by two developments absent in the rest of the region—the presence of not only the major but also the lesser-known denominations of the traditional Protestant church, and the added impact of the vocal evangelical sects as well. The anticlerical reforms of the late nineteenth century had opened the way for Protestant missionaries, but this movement really began to take shape after World War II. By the 1980s an estimated 22 percent of the population was associated with approximately sixty denominations. Their success appears based on two factors: (1) the degree to which the Catholic church has been discredited, and (2) the ethical and work values that form the core philosophies of the evangelical movements.

In the 1980s non-Catholic Christian churches have become more politically involved, receiving a boost with Rios Montt's presidency and the 1985 presidential candidacy of Jorge Serrano—both born-again Christians. This has highlighted a degree of tension between a morally conservative and aggressive Protestant church and a basically Catholic political environment divided among radical and conservative wings. Politically, the Catholic church retains considerable residual institutional strength and legitimacy and has, in the context of the insurgencies of the early 1980s, attempted to portray itself as the protector of the nation's indigenous communities. These unique developments, although not to be overstated, hold significant long term implications for Guatemalan society.

The Indian Population

Guatemala is a rural society with, not surprisingly, a large agriculturally based economy. Much of that economic base originates from the Indian communities in the highlands and border regions with Mexico. Known to most outsiders in the form of Mayan culture, the latter involves a geographical setting that historically incorporated southern Mexico to Guatemala and Honduras. The Mesoamerican or Middle-American culture thrived more than 1,000 years; along with the Incas of the Andean region and the Aztecs of Mexico, these cultures are viewed as the peaks of American Indian cultural development. Some of the more notable aspects of Mayan culture include: hieroglyphic writing, maps, a complex calendar, a very extensive knowledge of astronomy, and a rather elaborate—and, by modern standards, brutal—religious culture. This has in part generated the visible remnants of Mayan culture, which today can be visited in the Peten of Guatemala, and the Yucatan in Mexico. As a result of this strong heritage, Guatemala is an Indian society to the extent that even the modern or Europeanized portions of society refer to the nation's Indian heritage as a significant cultural backdrop.

The other by-product of this culture and far-away era is human: the well-preserved social and religious life of the Indians of Guatemala. Numbering approximately half of the current population, for centuries the Indians had constituted simple agricultural communities. The arrival of the Spaniards was a major change, with Indian culture adopting some trappings of Catholicism but otherwise remaining intact culturally. On an economic level, the Indian communities began to feel the pressure of modern economic development in the nineteenth century, but were in effect on the margins of Guatemalan political and economic life until the 1940s.

The last forty years have seen changes, most notably through communication and road-building, which more formally connected Guatemala's urbanized population with its Indian hinterland. Furthermore, since the 1940s, and most notably after the 1960s, the Indian population has been the constituency over which much of the nation's ideological and social battles have been fought. The political left has somewhat by default monopolized this terrain; its efforts have had mixed results due to the army's successful counterinsurgency campaigns, as well as the fact that Indian society remains very traditional in character. In the 1980s there has been a conscious attempt by Guatemala's central government to more actively integrate the Indian world into mainstream domestic economic development; such a move has admittedly been done for strategic considerations. The 1985 democratic elections also attempted to bring this community into the arena of national political participation.

3
Entrance into Modernity:
The Early Years

Introduction

It is important to remind readers in this turbulent last quarter of the twentieth century that the United States did not create instability and chaos in Central America; others did. Conversely, the United States cannot claim much credit for the brief interludes in which relative peace and prosperity were the basic characteristics of regional affairs. The Caribbean Basin's historical experience, out of which modern Guatemala has emerged, was at its beginnings a theater of conflict—long before Washington, D.C. had even been conceived. A backwater of colonial rule, Central America proper was an area where for some 300 years adventurers, smugglers, sailing fleets, lesser colonial elites, and a socially enslaved indigenous population formed the basis for Spanish rule. On the margins of cultural and technological progress, the region approached the nineteenth century with a less-than-distinguished basis for development.

Spain's domestic problems and ensuing bouts with liberalism in the 1820s generated a countermovement in Mexico and Central America. At the time, colonial Central America was essentially centered around Guatemala. A small-scale colonial community existed there, overseeing an environment that was in many ways unchanged from previous centuries. After a brief interlude during which Mexican ambitions toward Central America were stifled, in 1823 the United Provinces of Central America declared independence. This effort at regional unity, then as now, quickly self-destructed. Ultimately, five conservatively led nations that today constitute Central America proper were formed. In mid-1838, the federal congress declared that the member states were "sovereign, free, and independent political bodies," which set the groundwork for Guatemala's independence.

Guatemala's long search for institutionalized modern development has therefore been sought after for about 150 years. Until fairly recently, the process had remained inconclusive: It was only in the mid-twentieth century that the nation's leadership professed an inclination for giant steps toward change. But while the political history of Guatemala has been turbulent, it has not been one of endless and meaningless regime changes. In fact, it is tempting to highlight the considerable creativity of the nation's leadership to sustain a fairly static sociopolitical system well into the recent period. As elsewhere in Central America, the process of regime transition has neither been peaceful nor always spurred by a sense of enlightenment. In this context, instability has been an offspring of the region's often anti-quated attitudes toward purposeful governance.

The Historical Experience

The early years are colored with a string of personalistic figures whose tenures are punctuated by violent interludes. This is the era of dictators or traditional caudillos, primarily characterized by personal-istic politics, a never-ending cycle of intrigue, and a complete or authoritarian sense of governance. If there was turmoil and chaos at one extreme, Guatemala simultaneously also witnessed periods of relative order, albeit of a tyrannical sort. Four archetypes appear in Guatemala's political development: Jose Rafael Carrera (1844–48 and 1951–65); Justo Rufino Barrios (1873–85); Manuel Estrada Cabrera (1898–1920); and, as a transition figure between old and modern Guatemala, Jorge Ubico y Castenada (1931–44).

Governmental turnovers, unlike those depicted in Hollywood scripts, were brought about not for whimsical reasons but because of profoundly different visions of society. Although in retrospect the quality of government appeared not to differ from one vision to the next, national aspirations ultimately did zigzag toward the Guatemala of today. Those dictatorial regimes must be viewed in the context of the eithteenth and nineteenth, not twentieth century.

Until the early 1870s, Guatemala, like the rest of the Central American isthmus, was governed by an elite as much traditional in style as harshly conservative in philosophy. Still a matter of debate among historians, the Carrera period represented an era when the nation's two existing cultures—Indian and colonial Spanish—were sustained by opposing liberal or Europeanized flirtations with new economic and political ideas. The resultant tension built up to create the liberal revolts of the 1870s throughout the region. In Guatemala, its early expression was to be found under Barrios and the process brought to the surface a basic socioeconomic tension that has endured well into this century.

In the late nineteenth century, the liberal triumph contributed a whole new vision of economic development, where economic growth and exports spurred results of the kind the nation had not previously witnessed. It brought new sources of national revenue (coffee, in particular), began to change the infrastructural landscape (communications), undermined the influence of traditional institutions (particularly the Catholic church), created a foreign-oriented entrepreneurial elite, and introduced a new order that slowly began to affect the Indian majority with ultimately profound results.

The institutionalization of early liberal reforms ultimately evolved into what has been described as "republican dictatorships." Estrada Cabrera and, later, Jorge Ubico were "modern" in their appreciation of the importance of economic growth but subverted the republican political process that liberalism had brought from Europe. Stated briefly, a fictitious constitutional process was the surface feature of an ultimately superficial and poor public administration of resources, which in turn generated an arrogant governing political and economic elite, topped off by corruption at all levels of society. But change did occur despite these maladies, and for the first time a semblance of modern society developed. Under the trying circumstances of that era, it is less than surprising that authoritarian leadership dominated over the fragile appearances of democratic government and the realities of Guatemala's traditional society.

The character of Guatemala's government also promoted changes in two critical components of society: the church and the army. Reinforced under the earlier Carrera period, the liberal revolution signaled a setback for the church. Building on the anticlerical features of republicanism, the Guatemalan government moved against the church, both on political and economic levels, and subsequently broke the appearance of a parallel authority that the clergy had retained as a vestige of the colonial regime. The church maintained a certain moral authority at the local level, and perhaps became even more conservative than ever before—features that, to a degree, have been sustained into the modern era.

A modern state required an institutionalized national army, and a powerful leader needed an efficient one. Thus, the origins of Guatemala's armed forces date back to this important period. Prior to 1871 the nation did not have a reliable and orderly force, let alone one that could absorb technological and strategic developments emanating from Europe. To organize what had essentially been an urban militia, the Barrios regime and its successors brought in foreign military missions, first from Spain in the 1870s, and later from France, Germany, and, after World War I, the United States. In tandem, internal security

forces were established, along with the beginnings of a police. Professional training of officers became a priority, for which the Escuela
Politecnica was formed. This entire process was expanded after World
War I. By the time Jorge Ubico held office in the 1930s, the armed
forces had not only visibly been professionalized, but were now the
cement that held the government together.

A discernible trend toward economic modernization, affecting most
significantly the urbanized class, added a new element in society. In a
sequence of events since duplicated several times in Central America's
last decade, socioeconomic transformations coupled with excessive
political control created the chemistry for a potentially explosive
reassessment of the character of society. The political question that
Guatemala has confronted since 1944 has been whether to promote
change by radically modifying the conservative character of society,
or by promoting an evolutionary process. Unfortunately for Guatemala, to arrive at the 1985 electoral decision toward orderly evolution,
the nation first had to endure the revolutionary aspirations of the late
1940s and early 1950s, and then subsequently survive through years of
increasing political, if not societal, disorientation.

The Ubico Era

Although the tenure of each of Guatemala's caudillos was unique,
one thread that links them together since 1871 is that they came to
power by subverting the constitutional process without, ironically,
replacing it. The most successful of these leaders restored a facade of
order to the nation. However, the rule of Jorge Ubico (1931–44) was
the most instrumental in laying the foundations for a modern state,
thereby ushering the nation into a new age. Assuming power following
a brief period of considerable political uncertainty, Ubico created a
new role for the armed forces in society, modified financial management of the government, and upgraded the nation's foreign policy
relationships.

This important era can be divided into two periods. From approximately 1931 to the mid-1930s (1936–37) is a phase that can be referred
to as the "progressive" years. The years from 1937 to 1944 comprise
a second phase most appropriately characterized by the use of *person-
alismo* and *continuismo* in maintaining undisputed control of the
nation; the former characteristic relates to the use of personalistic
politics, while the latter term refers to the extension of a term in office
by constitutional manipulations.

Ubico came to power in 1931 through a series of relatively free elections. His candidacy was supported by the Liberal Progressive Party, which he had founded in 1926, drawing its support from university students and other advocates of mild reform within Guatemala. In light of the manner in which his rule was to evolve, support from these constituencies was rather ironic. Drawing on the concern of the United States government (which questioned the constitutionality of Ubico's immediate predecessor), he assumed office for a constitutionally designated six-year term. The immediate goal of his administration was challenging: to overcome the nation's deep economic crisis. This ultimately entailed a restructuring of Guatemalan social, political, and economic life. However, by 1937 Ubico's initial whirlwind of activity began to wane as his priorities turned to the more traditional pursuits: power and wealth.

Through his early years of rule, Ubico developed an enormous base of popularity, attributed to an unprecedented "honesty campaign," which was designed to eliminate widespread public sector corruption. In this context, the Law of Probity was initiated in 1931, requiring public employees receiving a salary of over U.S. $200 per month, and any officials whose work included the handling of public funds, to publicly declare their personal wealth upon taking office. As a result, 1931 was labeled the "Year of Sacrifice," suggesting that a national campaign was required to put the nation back on its feet.

An unusual attempt at social reform was the 1934 Vagrancy Law, which required all citizens owning less than 15/16ths *manzanas* of land (an amount deemed insufficient to support a family) to work the larger *fincas*—the Latin American version of a plantation—thereby providing the opportunity for the population to earn an adequate income. While this kept the indigenous population fed and employed, the legislation obviously also sustained a cheap source of labor for agricultural interests. In the end, Ubico's moderate internal reform permitted a further centralization of government control and economic stabilization of the country.

Ubico's popularity soared in the outlying areas of Guatemala, among the ladino as well as the indigenous population. A series of inspection trips throughout the country were undertaken, designed to afford the local communities the direct ear of the president, restructuring the exploitative methods of previous governments. An aficionado of fast cars and motorcycles, Ubico's trips took on an Olympian character, were widely reported in the press, and in later years degenerated into propaganda shows.

If the old cliché is true that "power corrupts and absolute power corrupts absolutely," Ubico fell prey to this in the second part of his rule. His tenure became fueled by his own ego, which ultimately convinced him of his own invincibility. Through the use of a fraudulent plebiscite, he proclaimed himself president for another term (1937–43), insisting that he was bowing to the will of the people. In 1941, the constitutional order was rearranged to add an additional six years to his tenure as president. In attempts to further centralize control throughout the country, local mayors (*alcaldes*) were replaced by *intendentes* (managers appointed for political reasons)—all loyal to the rule of Ubico, thereby providing unwavering assurance that "ubiquista" policy would be implemented.

Without doubt, the years of Ubico's rule are remembered by his critics for the increasing involvement of the United Fruit Company (UFCO) and, more broadly, American interests within Guatemala. Based in Boston, Massachusetts, UFCO appeared on the scene in Guatemala in 1899 as the result of the consolidation of the Boston Fruit Company and the entrepreneurial activities of Minor Keith. During the Ubico years, in a combined effort between the International Railways of Central America (IRCA), and the United Fruit Steamship Company (both subsidiaries of UFCO), the Guatemalan transportation network expanded greatly. These and other economic activities proved lucrative for Ubico and his cronies.

Ubico's authoritarian preferences generated a feeling of respect for the Mussolini and Franco regimes in Europe, although Ubico viewed Hitler as little more than an upstart. But Ubico also was aware of the fact that the U.S. government was his and, by extension, Guatemala's largest patron. During these years Washington became concerned with the influence of Guatemala's extensive German-owned coffee producing community—an issue that rose to the surface after the United States' entry into World War II. American concerns were openly expressed, and Guatemala moved swiftly toward taking over German landholdings, which were a sizeable portion of the nation's export-earning lands.

The rule of Ubico expanded not only the role but also the degree of professionalization of the armed forces. This expansion had important repercussions both in connection with Ubico's downfall, and later with the preponderance of the military in succeeding governments through 1985. During his rule, Ubico introduced a formal political role for the military. The emergence of a modern officer corps, as guardians of the nation's institutions, changed the armed forces into a more integrated political force. This became quickly apparent in the early summer of 1944 when the junior officers were catapulted into a front-line political role.

4
False Alarm?
The Arevalo/Arbenz Experience

Introduction

In the face of widespread protests, manifested through massive demonstrations and a general strike in June 1944, Ubico stepped down. On July 1, a letter of resignation was presented and in an almost offhand way, Guatemala found itself in the beginnings of a revolution. Indeed, Ubico's resignation was prompted by the shock of his sudden realization that he was no longer viewed as the national savior—as his thirteen-year tenure appeared to suggest.

The two final blows to his years of rule were a major student-sponsored general strike and the petition by 311 prominent middle-class citizens and professionals, indicating a surprisingly broad degree of public disaffection with Ubico. These actions were followed by other strikes—in this instance supported by the capital city's business community. Ultimately, the restoration of the constitutional process and the general liberalization of political restrictions that had developed under Ubico became focal points for Guatemala's political opposition.

Misinterpreting the nation's desire for change, a new military junta assumed power when Ubico resigned. The junta's coordinator, General Federico Ponce Vaides, in effect sustained the political framework that had operated under Ubico. While a few minor reforms were enacted, widespread public protests continued, growing in volume. Frustrated by the response of the military leadership, the civilian opposition successfully capitalized on the growing rift within the armed forces between the senior officers and the younger products of the Escuela Politecnica. The convergence of interests of the latter with the opposition came to a head in the fall of 1944; the severity of government repression led to the October 20 revolt. This marked a new phase in Guatemala's political development. In conjunction with student and other public support, Major Francisco Arana (later joined by Captain Jacobo Arbenz) of the Guatemalan armed forces mounted a revolt against the senior officers.

This was not to be the only time a split would occur in the officer corps. In the early 1960s, discontented officers would split off to launch new guerrilla groups. And in 1982, the discredited Lucas Garcia regime was initially thrown out by the actions of the younger officer corps. Perhaps the most striking element in both the 1944 and 1982 episodes was that the junior officers showed a remarkable instinct for the necessity of protecting the integrity of the armed forces in the midst of growing societal disaffection with the army.

The October 1944 revolt generated a provisional government around a triumvirate leadership—Arana, Arbenz and Jorge Toriello Garriddo, a prominent civilian who had been an outspoken opponent to the previous regime. This transition team governed through the elections (previously scheduled and ultimately held in December 1944) and turned over the national leadership to the election's victor, Dr. Juan Jose Arevalo Bermejo. Arevalo, an intellectual and academic, had recently returned from many years in exile in Argentina where he had held a university teaching post.

Introducing Social Revolution

Arevalo's political philosophy was one of spiritual socialism. To use his language, his administration was to be a period attentive to the common man, showing a willingness to address challenging socioeconomic and political needs. These reforms were of a populist nature, with a strong urban labor component, and involved an expansion of the welfare state. In subsequent years, several important pieces of legislation were passed.

Arevalo undertook new initiatives in the area of health and sanitation, and instituted a radically different labor code that guaranteed the right to organize and strike. The nation's education sector also received attention. The government focused considerable efforts on the land question, particularly as it related to the then nebulous issue of titles and ownership. Enacted during this period was the Instituto de Fomento de la Produccion (INFOP), designed as a grandiose effort to provide credit and technical assistance to the small rural producer, with an eye also on more effectively integrating the large Indian highland community.

A more spectacular development late in Arevalo's term was the 1949 Law of Forced Rental. Although in the end little implemented, the law was designed to force unproductive land into use. The system involved a mechanism by which land-owning farmers with small plots could petition the right to use fallow acreage in neighboring estates, at a rental rate set by law.

Opposition to Arevalo's policies came from a variety of quarters, ironically from both the political left and right. The left was becoming increasingly well organized and vocal, with the government's efforts on behalf of labor further institutionalizing Marxist influences. For these and other militants, Arevalos' reform programs were too slow. For the more conservative portion of the community, Arevalo's political difficulties led to greater dependence on the untrustworthy armed forces (there were twenty-two military revolts during his tenure). This situation was made more difficult after the assassination in 1949 of Major Arana—the individual who had held the army in check on behalf of the president since 1945.

As widespread opposition to Arevalo's policies took root, disaffection was to be expressed through several aborted coup attempts, in addition to the creation of a coup "rumor mill" in Guatemala City. Thus, rumors of coup attempts fueled increased opposition to the regime, culminating in ever-increasing levels of instability. In light of the fact that the armed forces had essentially engineered the 1944 revolution, the military remained a key component within the Guatemalan political arena. In tandem, Arana exercised an increasing amount of influence within the government and a struggle for a power eventually emerged between Arana and Col. Jacobo Arbenz—the two military members of the initial triumvirate. This power struggle was to culminate with Arana's assassination, although Arbenz's complicity in this incident has not been proven.

The 1950 Transition

The Arevalo regime was not a communist one, as many of its critics have charged. However, it is clear that the Guatemalan government and major associated political groupings, if not society as a whole, were rapidly moving in that direction. The polarization of the environment became quite apparent just prior to, during, and after the 1950 elections. This unworkable chemistry ultimately created the conditions for the 1954 revolution.

The 1950 elections were contested by three candidates, with the two principal figures being Col. Jacobo Arbenz and Gen. Miguel Ydigoras Fuentes. Arbenz, a product of the 1944 revolution, was by then Arevalo's minister of defense. A nationalist at heart, his politics were decidedly not favorable to the old-line political and economic elites. He had an agenda of economic reform that was to sharply conflict with the large foreign-owned agricultural operations. Arbenz captured the support of the communist elements and, through a broad coalition of liberal and leftist parties, early on became the favorite to succeed Arevalo.

In turn, Ydigoras, Ubico's minister of public works, was principally supported by the nation's conservative factions. The atmosphere of the 1950 campaign was bitter and ultimately led to a less-than-free election process. In fact, toward the end of the campaign Ydigoras faced a warrant for his arrest, which sent him underground. Arbenz won by a large majority and unleashed four years of mounting chaos within Guatemala.

The Arbenz Experimentation

Much of the scholarly attention devoted to Guatemala has almost religiously focused on the 1944–54 period as the nation's "revolutionary years." This has generated two diametrically opposed visions of those years. On the reformist side of the argument, the literature has attempted to convince the reader of the following points: (1) the reforms that were enacted were necessary and of a democratic nature; (2) communists did not formally participate in either the Arbenz or Arevalo cabinets, but instead participated simply in the constitutional process; and (3) the regime rightfully proceeded to undertake an agrarian reform, but that in opposing the oligarchy, it ran into American economic or even imperialist designs. The culmination of this line of argument suggests it was the latter that destroyed Arbenz.

On the conservative side of the equation, the Arbenz reforms were viewed as a blatant attempt to destabilize the country and lead it not toward the formation of democratic society, but rather toward communist rule. The development in 1952 of the communist Partido Guatemalteco del Trabajo (PGT) as a major player in the government's push for not only agrarian reforms but also the collectivization of resources and production is looked upon as an indictment of the regime. And if that were not enough, the presence of Arbenz's Salvadoran-born wife—an active member of the PGT—in the inner circles of government provided a sense of the real philosophical orientation of the regime.

Not surprisingly, the events of these years have generated voluminous quantities of rhetoric. Complicating this analytical environment has been an added feature relating to the downfall of the Arbenz government: the role of the United States. The Guatemalan experience falls squarely in the middle of the Cold War, and, after 1952, within the purview of ardent Cold War warriors such as John Foster Dulles. Furthermore, the interaction of the American government and corporate policy, namely that of UFCO, has added volumes of statements. At the very least, the lore on this issue is considerable, if divided.

It is not the purpose of this study to attempt to establish whether or not the reforms enacted in Guatemala in the 1950–54 period were either of a democratic or communist character. They were definitely extreme by local standards and produced an increasingly chaotic and radicalized environment. However, most damaging to the Arbenz government in the final analysis were four factors: (1) the government's land reforms escalated to a series of expropriations against UFCO, which in turn further mobilized its friends in high circles of the American government; (2) Guatemala's internal political orientation generated a foreign policy most likely to damage its ties with the United States without obtaining much else for it—support of North Korea in the Korean War, pro-Soviet statements in the United Nations, and acquisition of arms from Czechoslovakia; (3) Arbenz's penchant for labor politics swung out of control and ultimately was not only under communist control, but through bitter strikes and other labor actions left the country economically impotent; and (4) the final collapse of the regime was much less due to the machinations of the CIA and its counterrevolutionary army, as is popularly believed— instead, Arbenz lost touch with his own domestic reality, and most notably that of the reaction of the armed forces, which refused to rally around his sinking ship of state.

The Aftermath

With open U.S. assistance, the Arbenz government was ultimately replaced by what was initially the ragtag rebel army of Col. Carlos Castillo Armas, in the form of a two-man junta; within days, Armas assumed full control of the National Palace. Once having established his predominance, Castillo Armas promptly suspended the 1945 constitution and repealed the Agrarian Reform Law of 1952, as well as the Law of Forced Rental. Much of the expropriated lands were returned to their former owners. The left-wing political infrastructure of the Arbenz state was replaced overnight by its right-wing variant.

Castillo Armas, ultimately confirmed by a plebiscite in October 1954, governed a troubled environment until his assassination in 1957. Following up on Arbenz's inclination to use harsh methods against opponents, the new government engaged in a purification campaign of the Guatemalan political spectrum. The El Comite de Defensa Nacional

Contra el Comunismo (National Committee for Defense Against Communism) took on responsibility to insure that the aims of this plan were in fact implemented. The 1956 constitution confirmed the new order, which, in general political and economic terms, held until 1982.

A number of salient features appear to have become institutionalized in this period. First, the armed forces command returned as the key factor in national life, but this time with an increasingly distinct political mission. In acquiring such a role, the military began to operate autonomously from previously allied civilian factions or parties. For the next three decades, the army would operate as the final arbiter of the system. Still, there is no doubt that the armed forces were to a degree traumatized by the events of 1954. After all, the army appeared to be on both sides of the battle. Who were the heroes and true Guatemalan nationalists? This further politicized the army of Guatemala.

Second, the modern party structure became institutionalized in this period, and most importantly began to generate modernized, somewhat "loyal" oppositions of a democratic type. The right-wing Movimiento de Liberacion Nacional (MLN) and the moderate Democracia Cristiana Guatemalteca (DCG) parties emerged in this post-Arbenz era.

Third, although the Marxist orientation was removed from the governmental agenda, this did not generate a full halt and reverse course toward earlier eras. Much of Guatemala's social institutional infrastructure (for example, the Institute for Social Security) that exists today is derived from the period covered in this chapter.

Fourth, the impact of Arbenz's leftist experiment was profound enough to leave scars on the ideological landscape, sufficient to make the "communist threat" a continuing issue to this day.

Finally, this period of the 1950s also introduces, as the critics of American policy in Latin America love to point out, a new era of American interest and involvement in Guatemalan affairs. These critics have been correct in suggesting that this involvement became singularly associated with the maintenance of the status quo, but they are wrong in continuing to believe that this logic governs U.S. interests in Guatemala to this day.

The July 1957 assassination of Colonel Castillo Armas by a member of his palace guard does not appear to have had political motives. But the situation did immediately create a political vacuum that was filled by two provisional administrations. In the subsequent October 1957 elections, unable to read the handwriting on the wall, the civilian minister of the interior under Armas, Miguel Ortiz Passarelli, was designated the winner in an electoral fraud that was immediately resisted by the population at large. Ydigoras, who had lost out in 1950 against Arevalo, rallied popular support through widespread and violent demonstrations to state his claim to these elections. The outcome of this conflict was a negotiated agreement to hold another election in January 1958. This time, Ydigoras won by a slim plurality.

5

The Lurch Toward Democracy:
Searching for Internal Order

Introduction

Adapting to societal change has not been a specialty of Guatemala's governing elites. Their counterparts elsewhere in Central America have not fared much better. Responding to the acquisition of political influence by new socioeconomic groups in society—in other words, modernization—has involved a difficult national process. For these reasons, the 1960s and 1970s are important for Guatemala because they represent an era of adjustments, and years of violent transformation.

This period reflects both continuity and change in which the nation's traditional political culture goes through a series of attacks from groups that develop powerful alternative visions of the nation—reformist and, in many cases, left-wing. But these challenges were not met with a peaceful expansion of the political system; instead, this national debate was to be fought in pitched political and violent terms, lasting into the mid-1980s. In retrospect, Guatemala's political situation was made more difficult because of a crisis of leadership; placed in a regional context, this became the basis of the crisis that destroyed neighboring Nicaragua and, to a lesser degree, changed El Salvador. Guatemala ultimately managed its crisis in a distinct manner.

As had become apparent under Arbenz, ideological influences—specifically, communist—took root and became features of the Guatemalan political landscape. While ideology had played a role in earlier eras, by the late 1950s it began to widen its societal reach. Under Ubico, fascism had already raised its head and generated a marginally increased influence for Italy and Germany in domestic affairs. The political salience of this development was limited, however, to Guatemala City's urbanized elite. In contrast, Marxist ideology in the contemporary era has had a very different impact on the political character of the nation.

Arbenz's successors have had to deal with the extraordinary stamina of communism and its devastating impact on the fabric of society.

37

Unlike fascism in an earlier era, communist influence originated in Guatemala's intellectual and labor elites and expanded its reach into the politically virgin territory of the Indian communities. Significantly, this ideological outreach has not grafted itself particularly well in the highland's traditional Indian culture. The conservative character of indigenous society and religion, and its well-placed suspicion of Guatemala's "other" (urban and modern) community, have generated less than overwhelming responses to insurgent appeals. Nevertheless, Guatemala's bouts with left-wing extremism have dominated the political scene and governed the battle to expand or restrict the nation's ideological spectrum.

Despite the nation's slow and painful modernization process, the late 1950s and early 1960s did witness the coalescing of modernized political parties. Previously, they had been essentially elite groups in competition with one another. Until the 1930s, this had traditionally meant the competition of anticlerical and free-trade liberals with traditionalist and conservative groups. But with Ubico's modernizing authoritarian style of governance, this era witnessed the passing of this traditional national debate. In its place, since World War II Guatemala has developed a political party environment marked both by its ideological narrowness and its high degree of personalistic politics. In addition, the nation's development of a multiparty system has been affected by the predominance of the armed forces in affairs of governance.

The Modernization of Political Parties

The democratic elections of 1985 would not have been possible without a competitive political party framework. That the latter evolved at all is significant in view of the nation's imperfect experience in this area. Free elections were rarely a key element of the political landscape of Guatemala. Since the last century, a change in regime had revolved primarily around a system of elite manipulation and conflict. This system began to change after World War I, spurred on by the institutionalization of limited electorate participation. During this period, Guatemala acquired new vehicles for political competition through inspiration from the nation's intellectual groups (themselves influenced by external ideologies) and the development of an emerging professional and urbanized class in the 1940s. Thus, Juan Jose Arevalo's 1945 election occurred under a relatively democratic constitution—the first such instance in the nation's history.

Despite the turbulent national development of the 1954–63 period, it is during these years that several enduring civilian political parties began to appear. Of these, the Partido Revolucionario (PR), the Movimiento de Liberacion Nacional, and the Democracia Cristiana Guatemalteca became part of an expanding political landscape, a process sustained through recent years.

The PR traces some of its earlier progressive roots to the Revolution of 1944 as a legal successor to Arevalo's Partido de Accion Revolucionaria (PAR). The latter party was superseded by the amalgamation of factions that occurred during the 1950 election of Arbenz. The PR made its appearance as a moderate reformist party in 1954, and unsuccessfully bid for the 1958 elections. Ultimately, it became the flag under which the civilian candidate Julio Cesar Mendez Montenegro won the presidency in 1966. By then, the party had made a tactical shift rightward in ideology, although not far enough to prevent its moderate constituency from being victims of both left- and right-wing attacks in the nation's growing cycle of violence in the 1970s and early 1980s. The party remained a political force in the 1970 elections; however, it ultimately lost due to electoral irregularities that led the Congress to confirm the MLN candidacy.

Moving closer to the military, in 1978 the PR joined with the Partido Institucional Democratico (PID) to support the moderately conservative and ultimately disastrous electoral ticket of General Lucas Garcia and Villagran Kramer—a political mismatch of the first order. The PR fared even worse in the 1982 elections through its participation in a fraudulent victory, ultimately aborted by a coup. Internally divided, by 1985 the party had become a losing junior partner of an upstart party, the Partido Democratico de Cooperacion Nacional (PDCN).

The MLN has remained at the heart of ultraconservative politics in Guatemala for a quarter of a century. Its image, affected over the years by reports of affiliation with myriad conspiracies, has been tainted. A product of Castillo Armas's right-wing Partido de Unificacion Anticomunista (PUA) and subsequent Movimiento Democratico Nacional (MDN), the MLN party was reorganized by Mario Sandoval Alarcon, who has remained its major force.

The MLN contested the 1957 elections by stealing the first balloting and then losing the subsequent second round in early 1958. With a constituency representing wealthy agricultural-based and business elites, the MLN also developed early on a tradition of violent anticommunism, strong nationalism, and opposition to governmental interference in economic affairs. It has had over the years a degree of ideological compatibility with the armed forces and sympathizers in the United States. Yet, significantly, the MLN's basic philosophical features never made it a tool of the army (nor for that matter of the United States).

This tension with the armed forces grew more extreme in the 1970s as a new breed of military officer governed Guatemala and instituted marginal economic reforms that were viewed as anathema by the MLN's conservative economic constituency. In the mid-1970s friction with the military on political and economic issues erupted into formal political fights. During this period, the MLN was part of an increasingly unstable governing coalition—in the 1970 and 1974 elections, the MLN participated in a coalition with the PID. By 1978, outgoing President Kjell Laugerud's decision to ally the PR with the PID led to the defection of the MLN from governing circles. Its relations with the armed forces command was further strained in 1982 when the presidential elections were clearly stolen in favor of the government's military candidate. At that juncture, the MLN joined with the DCG and others to clamor for nonfraudulent elections. To some critics' surprise, the party actively participated with a somewhat rejuvenated cast in the 1984–85 electoral opening toward civilian, democratic rule.

The DCG also dates to the 1950s. Over the years it has shifted to the middle and the progressive side of the political spectrum. However, the DCG has remained within the established and "legal" portion of that spectrum (defined as having no links to guerilla movements) ultimately gaining the presidency in 1985.

The DCG's constituency initially grew slowly with the development of rural peasant and cooperative leagues, and a marginal social awakening on the part of wealthy rural businessmen and landowners. Contrary to the implications of its name, the links with the Catholic church's hierarchy were kept quite distinct. By the late 1960s, the DCG showed internal tension between those favoring radical reforms and others satisfied to pursue goals within the existing electoral framework. The party participated in its first presidential election in 1970, but in its aftermath began to suffer from a campaign attacking its perceived radical or even "communist" ideological preferences. As part of an electoral coalition in 1974, it supported the candidacy of a member of the military, General Rios Montt, a figure who was to reappear on the political scene in connection with the 1982 coup. In the interim period until 1982, the DCG suffered extraordinary casualties; a considerable portion of its leadership was sent underground or simply assassinated. Other parties, such as the leftist Frente Unido de la Revolucion (FUR), also suffered similar attacks in this period.

As elsewhere in the region, Christian Democracy has generally represented more of a pragmatic political program than strict ideological principles. In Guatemala, it has done so not out of cynicism but simply from a desire to survive, build a centrist-reformist constituency, and, ultimately, attain power. The DCG has viewed itself as a movement that attacks the perceived indifference of the conservative elements for social issues, while representing itself as a purposeful alternative to the radicalism of the left. Its Catholic character has operated more as a philosophical or moral framing than as offering an explicit theological association—an important distinction in modernizing Guatemala, where a large minority of the nation is of the Protestant faith. The vague notion that the DCG has attempted to represent a reconciliation of seemingly contradictory concerns and interests of conservative and left-wing elements ultimately has been shared by other political groupings and was a critical ingredient in the 1985 democratic elections.

In the final analysis, there are several key ingredients imperative in the development of a multiparty political system and, ultimately, a democratic environment. Perhaps the most important characteristic is the ability to make concessions in order to build and sustain political coalitions, strike bargains and reach acceptable compromises. Historically, Guatemala's political elites have not demonstrated a desire to take the necessary steps to forge a national consensus. Instead, these groups have tended to view political affairs in terms of a "winner take all" system, blocking the path toward any form of agreement. The development of a democratic environment has had to overcome the violent features of Guatemalan society.

The Culture of Violence

The modernization of the political party system has operated under a panoply of military regimes—the most common and enduring feature of Guatemala's entire political experience. The 1960s and 1970s added a new challenge: destructive insurgency movements, ultimately countered by right-wing expressions of violence. Still a concern in the 1980s, left- and right-wing rural and urban violence has represented a deadly counterpoint to the development of moderate political forces, which some of the aforementioned parties have represented. The patterns of violent activity that ensued acquired an institutionalized apparatus in the mid-1960s with a rural insurgency. The insurgency movement's failure later in the decade ultimately produced a shift in tactics: Violence moved into urban areas. Following a period of decline in the early 1970s, the insurgency took on a dramatic and vicious turn in the late 1970s, suggesting a society spinning increasingly out of control. We will return to this idea in later chapters.

The ideological content of this armed opposition has been predominantly of a Marxist-Leninist nature, even though the initial spark of development for these guerrilla movements was a 1960 aborted military coup. Left-wing groups drew much of their leadership from within the country's student community and, to a lesser degree, the trade union movement. Ties with external elements have existed all along, although relationships with established governments (the Soviet Union, Cuba, and, in recent years, Nicaragua) have remained essentially covert. Thus, there is no doubt that under the Arbenz regime, the PGT fronted for, and collaborated with, communist bloc interests.

The 1960s insurgency developed as a backdrop to the then-emerging Castro regime in Cuba and, later, the export of guerrilla warfare throughout the region. The first major insurgency group (Fuerzas Armadas Rebeldes—FAR) adopted Che Guevara's "foco" tactical concept, the somewhat ill-fated idea that suggested that through rural organization, guerrilla "focos" could defeat a regular army, bring down a military regime, and thus avoid having to develop a widespread revolutionary army of their own. (On this note, it should be recalled that Che lived in Guatemala under Arbenz and worked as an agrarian reformer; when the government fell, he ultimately found his way to Mexico where he met Fidel Castro.)

The restructuring of the armed left in the mid-1970s permitted its reappearance as a multiheaded insurgency. The latter coalesced in early 1982 into the Unidad Revolucionaria Nacional Guatemalteca (URNG). By then, all main guerrilla groups openly professed Marxian objectives, to be accomplished through a total transformation of Guatemalan society. One of the factions, the Ejercito Guerrillero de los Pobres (EGP) professed such a strong allegiance to the "foco" theory that it featured an outline of Che's bearded head and beret on its banner. To reach this point, the Guatemalan insurgency benefited over the years from discreet support from Havana and, indirectly, Moscow.

In the 1960s, Guatemala fell within the "active support" category of insurgent forces that Cuba was to cultivate, with Soviet acquiesence, as opposed to working with more orthodox communist parties. Then, with the Sandinistas becoming the most salient regional revolutionary experience, a network developed after 1979. Fidel Castro, already involved in revolutionary management consulting with Nicaragua's and El Salvador's leftist groups, encouraged the Guatemalans to follow the type of coordinated strategy successful in these neighboring countries. In 1984, Sandinista defector Miguel Bolanos Hunter suggested that following El Salvador, Guatemala was to be the next revolutionary situation to be cultivated by the Caribbean Basin's network of fraternal revolutionary movements.

Guatemala's political difficulties have had to overcome enduring dangers not only of the left but also of the right. This became increasingly apparent as each end of the political spectrum mutually reinforced their uncompromising and destructive character. Thus, from the early 1960s onward, these ingredients coalesced to steer the nation toward civil war. The campaign against communism that ensued in the aftermath of the Arbenz era ultimately evolved into political violence against a broader leftist community. In the end, vigilante groups were credited with terror against individuals simply suspected of seeking social justice or even moderate reform. Furthermore, by the late 1970s and early 1980s, political motivations for killings were to overlap with violence from a broadening petty criminal element in a society approaching the brink of anarchy.

With good reason, much has been made of the apparent collusion in the above events between the government and right-wing paramilitary groups. But these linkages have at times been exaggerated in suggesting that a succession of Guatemalan governments have in fact been the prime executor of these bloody policies. It is more likely that the governments, having launched anticommunist cleansing campaigns in the 1950s and counterinsurgency campaigns afterward, did not effectively contain, or were at times philosophically opposed to, the extralegal efforts undertaken on behalf of these campaigns.

The development of special relationships between conservative anticommunist political parties (such as the MLN) and the armed forces in the last three decades is not surprising considering their concordant political and ideological views. However, this has not been true in all matters of governance. In fact, it is more than likely that differences regarding economic matters might have made right-wing civilian groups even more intransigent than the military at varying points in time. In the 1960s, the appearance of such groups as Mano Blanco (White Hand), Ojo por Ojo (Eye for Eye), or the Consejo Anticomunista de Guatemala (Guatemalan Anticommunist Council) suggests that right-wing groups were emboldened by the expanding and successful army counterinsurgency campaign, but remained frustrated by the inability of civilians to respond to each instance of guerrilla violence. Thus, violence was never abated, the threat from the left continued through the 1980s, and, in the end, Guatemala acquired a number of very damaging epithets on the international scene.

From this scenario Guatemala's troublesome and widely publicized human rights image emerged. The literature is, as it should be, extensive and critical. But we should judge today's Guatemala fairly, not against a standard that the rest of the world cannot readily meet, but rather against the horrendous situation of an earlier period—and in the context of current political trends.

It is counterproductive to make sweeping generalizations about a "regime of terror" (Latin American Democratic Lawyers Association) or suggest that the Guatemalan military has "created a nation of widows and orphans" (*Bitter and Cruel*, Lord Avebury and Anthony Lloyd). Guatemala, like the rest of Central America, has been plagued by kidnappings, assassinations, and disappearances—indeed, a sad fact which has affected thousands of lives. But almost every political actor in Guatemala (including insurgents and terrorists of the left) shares the blame for this situation. There are few clean hands; it is perhaps deceitful for critics of successive Guatemalan governments to imply either that left-wing groups are not the cause of any violence in Guatemalan or that because "government" forces have been statistically responsible for more violent acts, their progressive opponents have somehow been more virtuous. In order to more clearly understand the origins of this difficult environment, one needs to examine three succeeding administrations: Ydigoras, Peralta, and Mendez Montenegro.

Ydigoras and the Birth of Insurgency

Ydigoras Fuentes's administration (1958–63) was profoundly influenced by the Cuban revolution. But, in the end, it was Ydigoras's own level of political incompetence and widespread corruption that brought this period to an end. To add to these difficulties, under his tenure the armed forces experienced a series of internal convulsions that suggested that the nation's major institution was under severe stress. The task of reversing this trend fell upon Ydigoras's successors in the late 1960s and 1970s. General Peralta, who succeeded him in 1963, began this difficult process of institutional and political reconstruction.

Ydigoras was, in many ways, the product of another era. He had been at one time Ubico's minister of public works and had survived subsequent periods of reformist confusion. Several times he had presented himself as the opposition candidate, and was therefore quite insistent in claiming that elections were stolen away from him. Ultimately, it was the absence of a strategic concept of governance, excepting gross mismanagement, that led Ydigoras into costly national adventures.

The first of these is significant because it ties Cuban and Guatemalan developments closely together. With Fidel Castro in power in Cuba after 1959, attempts to remove him proliferated. One of these efforts, sponsored by the CIA, involved the use of Guatemalan territory to train a force of Cuban exiles. Ydigoras's approval of this plan was strongly opposed on nationalistic ground by some of his fellow military officers. They in turn revolted and took a small contingent of the army with them into rural areas, meeting up with then-marginal insurgency groups. The upshot of this incident generated a major military campaign that crushed the original minor military revolt, but did not succeed in eliminating the other insurgents. In fact, the first formal left-wing guerrilla groups (such as the FAR and Movimiento Revolucionario–13—MR–13) appeared at first to proliferate and subsequently gain strength in the eastern portion of the country; one of these groups was headed by Arbenz's former minister of defense, Carlos Paz Tojada. In response to the growing number of combatants, with American technical assistance Ydigoras engaged in a more widespread counterinsurgency campaign, destroying the early wave of insurgent groups.

These difficulties generated several other challenges. Some came from within governing circles, such as the November 1962 air force dominated coup attempt. Other threats originated from outside the country and brought back old enemies. Former president Juan Jose Arevalo announced his desire to return to Guatemala. Living in Mexico, the former chief executive represented everything that Guatemalan conservatives feared and hated. His imminent arrival led to divisions within Guatemala's governing elite, with some supporting Arevalo's return and possible participation in future elections and other opposing such "heresy." In any event, the armed forces command moved against Ydigoras and sent him packing to Nicaragua.

This coup of March 1963 appears to have been a relatively amicable affair; the new strong-man, Colonel Enrique Peralta Azurdia, was at the time serving as defense minister. Although Arevalo's return precipitated Ydigoras's downfall, there are suggestions that, despite army pressures, the latter was in fact unwilling to depart in the midst of increasing confusion. Indeed, by then Guatemala was being governed under a state of emergency, and the insurgency was again on the upswing. The government's image as fat, corrupt, and uncooperative was becoming a possible international liability and clashed head-on with John F. Kennedy's White House, then in the process of instituting the reformist goals of the Alliance for Progress. The new Peralta regime wiped the slate clean by eliminating the useless constitutional framework of 1956, strengthening the army's hand in governance, and ushering in a new era of political affairs that in essence endured until 1982.

Peralta's Rule: "Restoring" Societal Equilibrium

In fomenting the 1963 coup, the growing instinct for self-preservation and modernization of the Guatemalan military is visible through a conscious attempt to rejuvenate the political climate. Upon Peralta's assumption of power, the 1956 constitution was dissolved and a new constitutional order was developed, concluding with a promised return to civilian rule in 1966. During this interim period, the military viewed its role as fourfold: (1) to stabilize the country by overcoming the challenges of the left and the squabbling among other groups in society; (2) to create a new and more durable constitutional order, to be introduced by the 1966 presidential elections; (3) to strengthen Guatemala's commitment to fight communism, preferably without the direct support of the United States; and (4) to reorganize the central government bureaucracy and engage in a limited campaign against overt corruption. These actions were viewed as necessary to instill a limited amount of domestic stability and tranquility.

While Peralta's rule was harsh (he initially sustained Ydigoras's state of emergency), a new societal equilibrium was attained. Fortunately, economic indicators remained strong and were further boosted by both the vigor of the new Central American Common Market (CACM) and an inflow of foreign investments. But in political terms, dramatic changes relating to the increasingly militarized character of society were necessitated to effectively combat stubborn guerrilla movements. This, in turn, modified the mission of the armed forces.

The military's increasing professionalism in the field transformed its original security function as a tool of the governing elites into a permanent and distinct political mission to protect society. The implications of this change were obviously significant not only for the political future of the nation but for economic development as well; the army began to engage itself in new spheres of activity, ranging from civic-action programs to national economic policy management and public works projects. This new form of activism on the part of the armed forces ultimately clashed with the views of the traditional political elite, who correctly assessed this new development as potentially affecting the traditional laissez-faire (or detached) role of Guatemalan governments.

Peralta kept his promise of returning the country to civilian government, but left to his successor the task of successfully prosecuting the return of insurgency. The political transition process ultimately involved more the appearance of democratic rule than such a reality.

The 1966 electoral contest had a rocky beginning when the PR candidate, Mario Mendez Montenegro, was assassinated in 1965 and had to be replaced by his brother, Julio Cesar. Voter participation rates were just over 50 percent, a figure that was to decline further in future years. And while Peralta handed the reins of power to a civilian politician in 1966, Mendez Montenegro was to be the exception rather than the rule; all other Guatemalan chief executives until January 14, 1986 (coinciding with the assumption of power by Vinicio Cerezo) were military officers.

The Mendez Montenegro Interlude

After years of instability, Montenegro's election brought hope. A certain reformist and socially conscious rhetoric appeared, and a desire to pursue conciliatory policies was initially enacted. In this context, attempts to clean up the nation's internal security and police forces were made, but with few positive results.

In fact, the character of violence took on a more institutionalized tone. An amnesty offered by the government to the insurgents was rejected. Furthermore, a skeptical opposition group among urban university and trade union groups increasingly became the target of violent attacks, with killings in urban areas becoming regular occurrences. In this context, extralegal paramilitary organizations began to surface as an adjunct to government security policy. To add to this generalized civil disorder, the guerrillas regrouped and engaged in a campaign to finance upcoming strategic offensives. Subsequently, there ensued a wave of kidnappings, which was countered by severe responses from the government's security forces and antisubversive elements.

Ultimately, the government won out and by 1970 the guerrillas (primarily the FAR) had been badly beaten. The man most responsible for this development, Colonel Carlos Arana Osorio, would in future years play an important political role. As Mendez Montenegro assumed the reins of power, Arana was recalled from his post as defense attaché in Washington to coordinate the military's counterinsurgency campaign. He was appointed military commander in the department of Zacapa, the stronghold of the rebel revolt.

With U.S. technical assistance, from 1966 to 1968 a successful, albeit fierce onslaught by the military was undertaken. The guerrillas were additionally weakened by two other principal factors: (1) the accidental death of Turcios Lima, former army lieutenant and de facto coordinator of the FAR, in a 1967 car accident; and (2) the inability of the guerrillas to coordinate tactics effectively and, at a strategic level, organize the civilian population into supportive groups. As a result of the collapse of the rural insurgency, the FAR campaign moved into urban areas—primarily Guatemala City. Thus, while the wave of insurgency began in the eastern region of the country, particularly in the Izabal and Zacapa departments, it eventually transited to urban areas. In contrast, the "second generation" of insurgency that would follow in the 1970s and 1980s would take place principally in the highlands and Quiche region, as well as the Peten.

The late 1960s counterinsurgency campaign was a violent one. In the period from 1966 to 1968, clashes between the guerrillas (FAR and MR–13) and security forces increased dramatically, as did the associated number of deaths, assassinations, and kidnappings. To compound the government's problem, the violence began to directly affect foreigners. U.S. military advisors were among the casualties, as well as the U.S. and West German ambassadors. All instances were credited to the FAR, although the disposition of U.S. Ambassador John Gordon Mein's case is less precise.

While the armed forces and its leadership became the masters of the scene, President Mendez Montenegro gradually descended into near abdication of authority and governmental responsibility. In the carnage that followed, even many of the president's own colleagues from the PR were assassinated. Finally, one bizarre incident in 1968 briefly shook the National Palace out of its stupor, and provides us with a sense of the near insanity that Guatemala's political environment had attained.

This involved the faked and bungled attempt to kidnap the Catholic archbishop of Guatemala City, Mario Casariego, well known for his conservative views. Members of the armed forces command promoted this incident with the desired hope of further discrediting the guerrillas, as well as the Mendez Montenegro administration. But the archbishop's less-than-full cooperation in this scheme backfired and forced Mendez Montenegro to act—thus temporarily strengthening the latter's hand in governance. This led to a mass dismissal of the government's senior security leadership, including the minister of defense, the head of the National Palace Guard, and, perhaps most notably, the head of the counterinsurgency's core campaign area, Colonel Arana, who was shipped out as ambassador to Nicaragua.

Despite its civilian and democratic facade, Mendez Montenegro's term of office concluded with a lopsided civil-military imbalance. By 1968, one could already discern the beginnings of military "developmentalist" regimes. The latter is really a reference to the process by which the military essentially stumbled into a plan of control over national affairs. These regimes were ideologically conservative in nature, and characterized by a near obsession with concern for internal security. Less sophisticated than the national security state implanted by bureaucratic authoritarian regimes in the rest of Latin America in the 1970s, Guatemala's military governments generated a program of governance based on a straightforward and simple plan that was to include a modern army presiding over a secure nation, leading to an internal equilibrium guaranteed by high rates of economic growth.

6
A False Equilibrium:
The Political Process and Violence

Introduction

The three presidents who occupied Guatemala's National Palace from 1970 through 1982 ushered in a period of relative political stability and economic growth, under a disguised formulation of democracy. These regimes were dominated by fraudulently elected presidents, each of whom had served their predecessor as minister of defense. Each regime relied upon a similar theory of governance: the tactics utilized against the revolt in Zacapa needed only to be politicized in order to guarantee societal stability. But by 1980, this increasingly artificial political construct led to a gradual disintegration of society, as exemplified by spiraling levels of violence perpetrated by almost all sectors within society. The final collapse of this equilibrium occurred in 1982, ironically at the behest of military elements.

In retrospect, the civilian regime of Mendez Montenegro was but a brief respite in Guatemalan politics; from 1970 to 1982 the military was to entirely control the political arena under a rubric that can be characterized as one of false equilibrium. Catapulted to a political role, Col. Carlos Arana was elected to the National Palace in 1970, in what was a fairly free election. Arana was succeeded by his minister of defense, General Eugenio Kjell Laugerud, despite the fact that in all likelihood General Rios Montt, the DCG-supported candidate, had probably won the March 1974 elections. Continuing in this vein, Kjell Laugerud was succeeded in March 1978 by the election of his minister of defense, General Romeo Lucas Garcia. Had it not been for the March 1982 coup, Lucas Garcia would have been succeeded in July of 1982 by his minister of defense, General Anibal Guevara, proclaimed the victor of the 1982 fraudulent electoral exercise.

The "Esquema Politico"

The Arana government began the construction of elaborate mechanisms of political management. A noted American specialist on Guatemalan affairs, Cesar Sereseres, has referred to this as the "esquema politico." Arana drew on the institutional and constitutional structures originally put in place by the Peralta regime (1963–65), although it remains unlikely that a formal "esquema" was ever designed; instead it is far more likely that the armed forces stumbled into such an arrangement. The political order that was to evolve was highly dependent on a tacit understanding among elements within the military, the political parties, and the private sector—the creation of a democratic facade that was to be marked by increasingly authoritarian politics, maintained through a structure of overwhelmingly fraudulent elections held in four-year cycles.

In this context, each of the three participating institutions sought a carefully balanced management of the political arena. Writing in *Report on Guatemala*, Sereseres suggests that to maintain this tenuously woven coalition, the Arana, Laugerud and Lucas Garcia regimes: (1) systematically co-opted symbols and institutions of representative government, (2) showed clear sympathies for private sector concerns, (3) further encouraged the growth and autonomy of the armed forces as the predominant institution within society, and (4) "neutralized" the leadership of independent or opposition organizations that could not be either co-opted, silenced, or bullied into exile.

The ultimate goal of these regimes was to negate the potential occurrence of threats to the political order represented by the labor and peasant populations, as well as to maintain undisputed control of the political process. Interestingly, this did not lead to a single form of political style. On the contrary, each regime between 1970 and 1982 had its own peculiar style of governance, and each developed new alliances by which to insure the maintainance of stability within society.

In this context, Arana tolerated the existence of reformist groups at the local level. For example, during 1970–74, the Frente Unido de la Revolucion and its founder, Manuel Colom Argueta, held the mayorality of Guatemala City. Laugerud made a tentative attempt to build popular support through a cooperative movement. Under Lucas Garcia the FUR was legalized as a national party, albeit only hours before its leader was gunned down in Guatemala City. Despite unique styles with respect to the management of the political order, all three administrations pursued a relentless campaign against a succession of urban and rural labor union groups. Furthermore, each also either tolerated or perhaps sanctioned extralegal activities—the famous "death squads."

The overarching concern of the government was to depoliticize segments of the population that could potentially organize themselves and create a threat to the societal order: labor unions, cooperative movements, university-based groups, and a broad range of rural groups. Characteristically, widespread violence became a requirement for maintenance of the system. Thus, as each new regime came to power, consistent attempts were made to find mechanisms that would secure the continuance of political rule and provide the government with a sustained legitimacy.

The decaying character of Guatemalan society created some dissent on the right, with gaps opening up between the army and its civilian sympathizers who were less than enthusiastic about the armed forces' preponderant role. It also created divisions within the military: the traditionalists, who supported the use of the "esquema politico," and a second group of officers, who supported a mildly reform-oriented posture. By the second half of the 1970s, General Ricardo Peralta Mendez and General Efrain Rios Montt—senior officers regarded as "politically reliable" by their colleagues—began to question the impact of the military's method of dominance of the political arena, as well as the measures being used to confront subversion and violence within the country. Nevertheless, the "esquema politico" was maintained.

The Army and the New Guerrillas

Previous governments had never completely destroyed the various guerrilla factions operating in Guatemala's vast hinterland. As indicated earlier, some shifted their field of activity to the urban areas. But by 1972 one could discern the birth of a "second generation" insurgency. This new wave proceeded more cautiously than its earlier brothers-in-arms and began generally by political organization rather than launching a frontal assault on the army. It took several years for this movement to mature in the Indian highlands. Just as the FAR's urban resistance fronts were rapidly declining in 1970, an initial cadre of the Ejercito Guerrillero de los Pobres emerged in the northern region of Ixcan and established itself in early 1972. Continued disaffection with a lack of political development within the nation only served to provide reservoirs of support for the insurgents. But ideological, geographical, and tactical differences blocked the consolidation of one predominant guerrilla group; instead, factionalism among the insurgents led to the creation of several groups, including the Organizacion Revolucionario del Pueblo en Armas (ORPA), EGP, FAR, and the MR–13.

External assistance for these groups grew most notably after 1979.

Although the precise amount of material assistance supplied to the insurgents via Managua and Havana is uncertain, political assistance from Fidel Castro was to ultimately have a large impact upon the guerrilla movements. Key in this regard was the 1981–82 agreement among the four largest guerrilla movements (FAR, MR–13, EGP, and ORPA) to unify the groups under the URNG banner.

An effective, albeit bloody, counterinsurgency waged in the highlands after 1979 generated violence in urban areas as well. Significantly, guerrilla cells were established in Guatemala City. But this violence was more than politically motivated. By 1981 it acquired a gruesome and senseless character.

Problems on the International Front

External developments served to add new problems to Guatemala's agenda. Most prominent among these were relations with the United States. Two problems developed in the mid-1970s that sent U.S.–Guatemalan relations into a tailspin. In the first instance, after approximately twenty years of steady military assistance flows, in 1975 the United States found itself caught in the middle of a territorial dispute between two allies.

Guatemala's long-standing claim over Belize heated up as the British colony neared possible independence. In this period, Guatemala adopted a threatening posture toward it and promoted its claim forcefully. Rallying a spirit of nationalism—already strong on this issue— the Laugerud administration upgraded the rhetoric regarding what was then British Honduras. Under pressure from the British government, the United States decided not to deliver any military equipment that London believed the Guatemalans could use in an invasion of Belize. While this action provoked negative sentiments in Guatemala City toward Washington, it did not prevent Guatemala from receiving military equipment from elsewhere, Israel in particular—a trend to be expanded in later years. Subsequently, too occupied with its own internal problems, when Belize acquired independence in 1982 Guatemala simply refused to recognize its legitimacy.

The second problem with the United States proved more serious, as its underpinnings were to plague U.S.–Guatemalan relations until the present period. The Carter administration took office in 1977 and human rights were catapulted to a major U.S. foreign policy focus. In its implementation, the administration's policy was to link U.S. external assistance to internal human rights record—and the policy applied most vociferously to Latin America. Guatemala, already a target of congressional attention for some years, was subjected to the full meaning of this new policy in 1977.

The nation's terrible human rights record was an easy target, but Guatemala's subsequent response was probably not the one intended by Washington; the policy demands were viewed as inadmissible by the Guatemalan government. Instead of backing down and negotiating an acceptable outcome with the U.S. government, Guatemala's historic tendencies toward nationalism as well as xenophobia led it to retrench and face its declining fortunes on its own. If the primary objective of the Carter administration was to force an improvement in Guatemala's human rights policy through a reassessment of its counterinsurgency campaign, the subsequent breakdown in relations did not affect the human rights record. In fact, in subsequent years it grew even worse. Left to their own devices, Guatemala's security forces chose to intensify the application of internal pressures.

International attention to Guatemala's turbulence was further fueled by several notable incidents: (1) the 1978 Panzos affair in which roughly 50 to 100 Indians were killed by Guatemalan military forces, and (2) the January 1980 siege and accidental burning of the Spanish embassy when security forces attempted to remove protestors. Following the latter incident, in which approximately 35 to 40 people were killed, Spain broke off diplomatic relations with Guatemala. This further galvanized European attention toward the nation's internal disorder and violence.

Compounding this record, in 1979 two prominent opposition leaders were assassinated: Manuel Colom Argueta, the former mayor of Guatemala City and leader of the FUR Party; and Alberto Fuentes Mohr, the former minister of foreign relations under Mendez Montenegro, as well as founder of the Social Democratic Party. Their deaths seemed to signify that no opposition that threatened the "system" would be tolerated, adding to the already discredited image of the country in the international community.

It was against this background of declining internal trends and increased international attention to the violence within Guatemala that the 1982 electoral exercise was held. In the two months preceding the March elections there were some 1,000 political deaths—an astounding level in a nation with a population, at that time, of only approximately six million inhabitants. In these troubled elections, the principal candidates were: (1) General Anibal Guevara, who had served as Lucas's defense minister representing the FDP, which included the PID, PR and FUN; (2) Alejandro Maldonado, representing the United National Opposition (UNO), which included DCG as well as MLN moderates;

(3) Mario Sandoval Alarcon, the undisputed leader of the MLN; and (4) Anzueto Vielman of the Central Autentico Nacionalista (CAN), an offshoot of the MLN. With less than 7 percent of the population participating in a hopelessly fraudulent exercise, the "official" candidate, General Anibal Guevara, was proclaimed victor.

The fraudulent election of Anibal Guevara confirmed the belief among some of the military's junior officers that Guatemala was going to face more of the same: corruption, inefficiency, extralegal violence, a growing death toll within the nation, stronger guerrilla movements, and further diplomatic isolation. Thus, three weeks after the 1982 elections, a coup was mounted by young officers concerned by the possible collapse of their own institution—and that of the nation as a whole. Following the resignation of Lucas Garcia, these young officers, respectful of authority, negotiated the creation of a three-man junta comprised of senior military officers. Within four months of the March 1982 coup, General Efrain Rios Montt, the unsuccessful candidate in the 1974 elections and a recently converted born-again Christian, assumed sole control of the National Palace.

7
Restructuring of the Political Arena: The First Steps

Introduction

The 1982 coup, sparked by the junior officers within the Guatemalan armed forces, was primarily concerned with three major factors: (1) a deteriorating political environment and ominous insurgency, (2) an increasingly discredited political and military leadership, and (3) an unfavorable international image. As indicated in the closing of the previous chapter, the initial three-man junta, installed by the junior officers, eventually gave way to a single leadership under General Efrain Rios Montt, a curious individual in Guatemala's political culture.

The Rios Montt regime and its advisory body, the Council of State, although originally applauded for its revitalization of the domestic political and security environment, was eventually to produce a scorecard of mixed results. But while the regime may not have met with success in all its varied initiatives, it was ultimately Rios Montt (and the head of his Council of State, Jorge Serrano Elias) who stood as chief architect of the strategic framework for the 1985 electoral process and return to democratic rule. Accomplishing this involved painstaking negotiations within the armed forces command.

The various components of this strategic framework were as follows: (1) the dissolution of the 1965 constitution, (2) the holding of Constituent Assembly elections on July 1, 1984, and (3) the newly elected 88-member Constituent Assembly was tasked with writing a new constitution and habeas corpus laws. The final electoral component in returning to democratic rule were the presidential, legislative, and municipal elections of November and December 1985; a full return to civilian rule was highlighted by the January 14, 1986 inauguration of Vinicio Cerezo Arevalo as president.

Tentative steps toward the rejuvenation of Guatemala's politics appear to have been conditioned by desperation. Suggestive of inherent strengths, Guatemalan political culture appears to have dug very deeply to find an alternative to the cycle of destruction prevalent since the 1970s. A move toward democracy was not the most natural step for Guatemalan society at that time, but it was the only one that offered hope. In addition, Latin America's overwhelming trend toward the restoration of democratic rule in the early 1980s provided a concrete example for Guatemala. Exhausted and dicredited, with nowhere else to go but national suicide, it took another tumultuous three and a half years to arrive at the end of the first step toward a positive restructuring of the political environment.

Characteristics of the Rios Montt Regime

Perhaps one of the most important contributions of the Rios Montt regime (aside from the strategic framework for the 1986 return to democratic rule) was a preliminary revitalization of the rural environment through a reorganized military management infrastructure. This new infrastructure launched a relatively successful counterinsurgency campaign—brought about in part by an appreciation of the political significance of community development. Most important in this regard were the use of civic action programs by the military, designed to win the "hearts and minds" of the rural population. Foremost among these programs was the controversial "bullet and beans" program, which eventually gave way to improved military relations with the civilian population. Another element in this strategy was an effort to create the equally controversial civil defense forces, which, utilizing the highland population, would provide yet another line of defense against the guerrillas. Later military administrations would continue to advance the concept of civic action programs; in the 1983–84 period, *polos de desarrollo* (development poles) were instituted in order to foster the repatriation of refugees back into highland areas.

An important component in the "normalization" of the Guatemalan environment was a marked decrease by late 1982 in the state of fear and violence, which allowed the repositioning of Guatemala's civilian urbanized leadership toward a more vital role in national affairs. This class within Guatemalan society was by then on the edge of extinction. Finally, as elaborated earlier, most important in this regard was the thrust of governmental policy in the 1982 through 1985 period: the construction of a viable framework for the introduction of democratic institutions. Although prone to fears of midcourse change (including the 1983 coup by General Oscar Mejia Victores), the recognized need for political reform and the military command's apparent desire to "civilianize" political affairs remained a constant feature.

The Fall of the Rios Montt Regime

Rios Montt's tenure was to last just a little more than one year; in August 1983 he was overthrown by his defense minister, General Oscar Mejia Victores. At the time, this change in leadership within the National Palace appeared to be a replay of events in the 1970 to 1982 period. However, in this instance fraudulent electoral exercises were not used to qualify regime change. And to the surprise of the international community, upon assuming office the new regime quickly assured the public that despite the change in leadership the nation would continue on its return to democratic rule.

Why then, was Rios Montt deposed? After all, there had been a significant decrease in random violence—at least at the beginning of his tenure—and, of equal importance, a framework for return to democratic rule had been laid out. During the years in which the Guatemalan armed forces held the reins of political power, a tacit alliance had been struck among Guatemala's powerful institutions, namely, between certain civilian political elements, the Catholic church, the private sector/economic elite, and the military. In retrospect, Rios Montt was unable to maintain this informal alliance; one by one, each of these institutions withdrew their support from the Rios Montt regime.

While Rios Montt's personalized appeal to integrity and traditional family values was refreshing in its originality and signaled the beginnings of a moral rejuvenation within Guatemala, it also served to earn him notoriety and disfavor among certain political classes. In a predominantly Roman Catholic society, his close association with the evangelical movement disrupted the regime's alliance with the church. Furthermore, his mishandling of the economic environment was to cost him the support of the private sector. Finally, and in a somewhat paradoxical fashion, his popularity and grass-roots support among the lower and lower-middle income groups was ultimately viewed by the army command as simply generating too much independence.

In this context, there were fears that a new caudillo was being born, over which few would ultimately have any control. Thus, it was this independence, rather than religious antagonism, that finally culminated in his August 1983 removal. In his last months of rule, Rios Montt's perceived hesitancy to fully articulate and move ahead with a democratic transition also prompted the armed forces to act. In fact, upon assuming power, statements from the National Palace indicated that the Rios Montt regime's fourteen-point plan for return to civilian rule would be fully implemented—only the leadership that would oversee the process was to be altered.

The Mejia Victores Regime and Return to Democratic Rule

Prior to the 1985 sequence of elections, the July 1984 Constituent Assembly elections were the most important structural component in Guatemala's drive to a democratic government. Installed on August 15, 1984, the Constituent Assembly set in motion a constitutional framework for political competition and reestablished a somewhat fragile process of national discourse and timing. If nothing else, and to the surprise of many, the July 1984 elections were themselves quite clean and the subsequent eighty-eight-member convention process was in fact ultimately brought to a visible threshhold in mid-1985 with the issuance of a new constitution. Although the original electoral timetable had been delayed several times, the agreement to return to civilian political life remained essentially unaltered.

To the above analysis one can add at least four elements that have served to shape the democratization process in Guatemala: insurgency and terrorism, human rights, the economy, and U.S. diplomacy. In practice, all the elements are interrelated. The human rights situation remains related to both the aftereffects of fighting a simmering insurgency campaign, as well as the severe economic crisis. The two combined suggest a degree of social malady bound to constrain Guatemala's ability to *rapidly* improve its human rights record. However, when looking at the trends since 1984 the number of abuses has decreased dramatically. One can perhaps judge Guatemala fairly, not against an abstract standard of Western society, but rather against the horrendous situation that had occurred only a few years prior in the context of present political trends. Obviously, even in the post-1984 period Guatemala has remained plagued by kidnappings, assassinations, and disappearances. In fact, trends during the 1985 electoral period were less than reassuring. The well-publicized assassination of leaders of the Grupo de Apoyo Mutuo para Familiares de Desaparecidos (Mutual Support Group—GAM), a leading Guatemala human rights organization, further served to exacerbate international concern in this matter.

Considerable speculation exists regarding violence. It is more than likely that every political actor in Guatemala shares some of the historical blame. There are few clean hands in this matter, although clearly in this political environment the destabilizing forces on the extreme left and right saw the most to gain in halting the nation's democratization process. Guerrilla activity by Marxist insurgents in the Peten region, northern Quiche, and Lake Atitlan remained a threat in spite of considerable successes by the armed forces in these two regions since 1982. In addition, urban terrorism against targets of all political persuasions remained a problem. Furthermore, in a replication of trends in other parts of Central America, tough government reactions to insurgent violence have conveyed an unfavorable reputation and generated appeals to international conscience against the use of "repressive tactics."

In the midst of this situation, the nation's economic viability became an issue and did in fact turn into a political variable. In decline since 1980, the economy in 1983–84 registered negative growth rates and disturbing signs of galloping inflation. Foreign investment came to a halt, strict foreign exchange and export-import controls were instituted, and the nation's overall ability to pay its bills—let alone its foreign loan committments—hit some tense moments. Overall, the limited growth potential of the nation's traditional export commodities, combined with both in-country and regional political risk factors, generated a faltering economic environment.

The mishandling of the economic environment by successive military regimes forced a break and subsequently gave way to a conflictual relationship between the military government and the private sector. The latter, organized under the umbrella group CACIF, has come to wield a significant amount of political clout. The spring 1985 showdown between these two groups over government-sponsored tax laws, in which the government eventually backed off its position, only served to highlight how taut the economic policy domain had become. It also demonstrated an ability by all parties concerned to stave off a major political crisis. One public policy instrument that came out of this near exchange of blows was the "National Dialogue."

The National Dialogue was a somewhat transparent attempt by the Mejia Victores government to buy political time through a commission-type exercise; as a result of this maneuver, the National Dialogue came up with a series of nebulous economic policy recommendations. Some of these, such as reductions in government and state agency expenditures, had a chance of being adopted. Other suggestions, including several related to tax adjustment questions, continued to be the target of negotiation among the various forces that constituted dialogue—with the government, CACIF, the labor confederation, the National University of San Carlos, and principal political party figures being the leading players. At the same time, most outside observers suggested that the implementation of a tough package of economic medicine at a delicate period in Guatemala's political life might be less than desirable. Thus, while the restoration of civilian rule was the ultimate objective, such sentiments clearly underlined the fragile balance that existed between the nation's democratic timetable and its economic and social fabric.

The role of the United States in Guatemala's return to civilian democratic rule should be the subject of a study in and of itself. It is a complex issue and operated in the broader regional context of Washington's campaign to stabilize and democratize Central America. Suffice it to say that when the Reagan administration came into power in early 1981, it was faced with a Guatemalan situation not likely to have any sort of appeal for U.S. public and congressional support. Fortunately for Guatemala, it remained a sideshow in American perceptions while El Salvador and later Nicaragua were the center of attention in the 1981–84 timeframe. However, during this period when Guatemala received limited attention in Washington, perceptions were so negative that the freezing of U.S.–Guatemalan relations instituted under Jimmy Carter thawed only very slowly.

Talk of a timetable for democratic government under Rios Montt, confirmed by the Mejia Victores regime, provided the first useful political ammunition to even attempt to push for a renewed positive American orientation toward Guatemala. A change in U.S. ambassadors likewise provided an opportunity to improve the tone of personal relationships with the Guatemalan government. The message from Washington became relatively clear: We cannot help you, on an economic level or otherwise, unless Guatemala demonstrates some positive steps toward democratic governance and all that such a transition implies in the human rights arena.

The Reagan administration did not have an easy time of it. Successive congressional visits in the 1984–85 period were often delicate exercises involving fundamental American distrust of the Guatemalan military officers involved in bilateral discussions. Guatemala's efforts did receive a sympathetic ear from the more conservative circles in the United States, although even there practical offers of support remained predicated on a Guatemalan ability to continue implementation of a plan for political opening. The disbelief that Guatemala appeared committed to a democratic timetable was to a degree carried into the aftermath of the December 1985 elections and suspicions that the new government was little more than a facade for old unchanged political traditions persisted.

The Constituent Assembly elections of 1984 provided the first concrete indication of Guatemalan commitment. By 1985, Guatemala's standing slowly began to rise, as demonstrated by the significant jump in the U.S. foreign assistance contribution (see Table 4). In retrospect, the fact that the Guatemalan army was able to turn around the insurgency essentially on its own, albeit brutally, avoided Washington's deeper and more controversial involvement in that nation's domestic affairs. When it came time to pass judgment on Guatemala's political opening, American policy was relatively unencumbered by the type of complications that appeared in Washington's relations with El Salvador, Honduras, and Nicaragua. Thus, the American role in Guatemala has, in this delicate point of transition, been positive and very important.

Constituent Assembly Elections

In 1984 and 1985, several political and economic developments within Guatemala helped to shape and nurture the nation's fragile democratic spirit. Perhaps the most important component in this regard was the election of a Constituent Assembly on July 1, 1984. In retrospect, various assessments of Guatemala's previous elections have been accurate; such exercises have often served as nothing more than a veneer to qualify a series of less than representative governments. As such, the predictions for the 1984 elections were for widespread voter fraud, as well as rampant voter apathy. Much to everyone's surprise, a stunning 72.66 percent of the eligible electorate turned out to vote in what was hailed as the first nonfraudulent election in many years, overseen by an autonomous Supreme Electoral Tribunal established under the Rios Montt regime.

A total of eighty-eight members were elected to the Constituent Assembly; twenty-three national deputies were chosen from a national list and sixty-five local deputies were selected from district lists. Electoral districts geographically coincided with Guatemala's twenty-two departments, excluding the disputed territory of Belize and the department of Guatemala was itself split into two districts: the metropolitan area, Guatemala City proper; and the municipalities within the district area surrounding the metropolitan area. Therefore, there were twenty-three electoral districts in total.

For the national elections, in districts electing three or more deputies, the proportional representation system was used, based on the geographical distribution of the population. In contrast, for local elections in which only two deputies were elected, an absolute majority system was utilized. A total of 1,179 candidates participated; 300 candidates vied for the twenty-three national seats and 879 candidates for the sixty-five local districts. The entire electoral and ballot-counting procedures were designed to eliminate the opportunity for fraud. Although the elections proved to be a success in this regard, the actual implementation of this system was rather elaborate and, particularly in terms of ballot counting, lengthy; final vote counts required nearly a full month to be generated.

In total, seventeen political parties, two formal coalitions, and three civic committees (who, due to logistical problems, were unable to attain party status) participated, with diverse ideological motivations ranging from the extreme right to the center of the Guatemalan political spectrum. By law, any parties tied to the guerrilla umbrella organization, the URNG, were denied participation in the elections, effectively excluding involvement of the extreme left-wing portion of Guatemalan politics. Ideologically, the major unifying threads among the participating parties were varying shades of an anticommunist posture and considerable nationalism, which have long been traditional features of Guatemala's political parties.

The outcome of this electoral exercise proved to be a resounding victory for the nation's centrist parties: the newly formed Union del Centro Nacional (UCN) gained twenty-one deputies, and the DCG garnered twenty deputies. Although by popular vote results the DCG emerged the clear leader, the MLN-CAN coalition of the extreme right captured the largest number of deputies, with twenty-three. The apparent discrepancy between popular vote results and assignment of deputies per party was due to the fact that rural area districts involved fewer votes per elected deputy. Thus, since the MLN captured an overwhelming majority of rural areas, the party received a larger proportion of deputies.

An unusual outcome in these elections was generated by a civic committee based in Quezaltenango, in the Indian-populated highlands. The Organizacion Campesino de Accion Social (OCAS), led by Mauricio Quixtan (a 1985 vice-presidential candidate), made Guatemalan history as the first indigenous official elected to national office. In the interim, Quixtan has become a seasoned, if somewhat offbeat political figure. Indigenous representation was further enhanced by five other deputies elected under the DCG banner. The symbolic importance of the OCAS victory perhaps outweighed any real political significance in terms of a realignment of forces in the country. But the presence of indigenous representatives in the Constituent Assembly was important in suggesting a mild opening of traditional, nationalized, urbanized political affairs to a broader rural and traditional constituency.

Constituent Assembly Deliberations

Sworn into office on August 15, 1984, the Constituent Assembly was scheduled to complete its work within a ninety-day period. Clearly the assembly fell short of its goal; the new constitution was not issued until late May 1985. As a result, the electoral calendar was delayed several times, although the concept of democratization was sustained throughout this period. Speculation has abounded as to the reasons for the assembly's delay; several issues must be taken into account.

Clearly, deliberations proceeded at a snail's pace partially due to party jockeying, which immediately embroiled the assembly process. Operating in something of a legal no-man's land (the 1965 constitutional order had been dissolved in 1982), and constrained by the political realities dictated by the military government, procedural and conceptual concerns in writing the new constitution took weeks, if not months. A rotating assembly leadership was ultimately agreed to, with the DCG, UCN, and MLN taking turns as president. Conceptually, the design of a new constitutional document hinged on a number of basic concepts relating to ownership, state perogatives, legal rights, social responsibilities, and veiled references to military control. These were all serious matters heading the assembly several times to the brink of chaos.

As it kept a close eye on the anticipated 1985 elections, the assembly became a highly politicized body. Through their elected deputies, various political parties used the assembly as a forum through which party platforms were introduced. In addition, bickering within the assembly was widespread, coalitions were formed and broken, and political jockeying continued as the 1985 campaign season approached.

In tandem with these assembly deliberations, the DCG, led by Vinicio Cerezo Arevalo, emerged as perhaps the strongest party. Organizationally and electorally weakened over a dispute involving electoral power sharing and other matters, the conservative MLN-CAN-PID coalition collapsed. The UCN formed·a three-way coalition with PNR and the PR at the beginning of the Constituent Assembly, but that too floundered during assembly meetings. The collapse of this coalition led many observers to suggest that the UCN had lost its initiative and early dynamism. In turn, the PR formed a coalition with the newly formed Partido Democratico de Cooperacion Nacional, led by Jorge Serrano, and the PNR decided to go it alone.

The Constituent Assembly process was also slowed by several social factors. For example, just as the assembly process got under way in August it was revealed that a deputy of the Frente de Unidad Nacional party (FUN), Santos Hernandez, was illiterate and therefore ineligible to participate in assembly proceedings. Although his party demanded a replacement, the assembly refused to remove him. Subsequently Hernandez left his party to join the MLN party ranks; in October, he was assassinated. Although Hernandez's death was an isolated event, this episode brought to the fore speculation regarding the educational levels of the deputies entrusted with the delicate mission of drafting a new constitutional document. Knowledge of constitutional law, a field of specialization in which few are well versed in any country, had not been a criterion for election to the assembly. This factor, coupled with historical weakness of constitutional procedures in Guatemala were but two contributing factors that curtailed both the depth and speed of deliberations.

It was also argued that the deputies intentionally benefited financially from the lengthy constitution drafting period. Salaries were quite high: approximately 3,000 quetzals per month (which, even with declining exchange rates, was U.S. $1,500–$2,500 dollars), a large financial reward for the deputies' travails. Obviously one can only speculate on this point, but the Constituent Assembly was certainly a salient financial expenditure. Parenthetically, the assembly did not dissolve itself once the new constitution was issued, but remained a deliberative and salaried body until the inauguration of the new civilian government on January 14, 1986.

The 1985 Constitution

Issued in late May 1985, the new Guatemalan constitution never received entirely favorable reviews. However, due to time delays encountered in drafting it, the document was at minimum greeted with a sense of relief; yet another critical component of Guatemala's democratization process had been successfully completed.

In accordance with Latin American traditions, the constitution is lengthy, detailed, and cumbersome. It contains several new articles regarding congressional-legislative relations, human rights, and judicial mechanisms. Nevertheless, two major criticisms have been directed at the document: (1) it is a less than satisfactory replica of the 1965 constitution, and (2) the document contains several articles that might be construed as being in conflict with each other. Thus, it was widely speculated that the new constitution was designed to be amended and edited by the Congress, which was to be elected in late 1985.

With regard to human rights concerns, the 1985 constitution delineated some new territory. Article 46 established the new principle that, with regard to human rights, international law would be predominant over internal Guatemalan law. This established a precedent, namely that Guatemala would be willing to subject its human rights records to the judgment of the international community. Additionally, Articles 273–75 called for the formation of a human rights commission and an attorney general for human rights, both designated by, and responsible to the National Congress. Specific laws governing the commission were later drafted by the Constituent Assembly.

Interestingly, the powers of the vice-president of Guatemala were greatly expanded (Articles 190–92). He has been given the capacity to participate during the sessions of ministers (the Cabinet) with both voice and vote. Prior vice-presidents, while able to attend cabinet sessions, could not participate in any form; his presence at these sessions was viewed as symbolic. Thus the extension of the vice-president's power has twofold meaning: (1) he has become the de facto vice-chairman of the cabinet, and (2) his vote in cabinet sessions gives increased authority to governmental decisions. It also implies a collegial, political decision-making process, a presidential team, all with attendant political ramifications.

Revisions of the judicial system were also outlined. Prior to the 1985 constitution, a Court of Constitutionality had been established to rule on specific cases being called into session by the chief justice of the Supreme Court. Changing gears, a Court of Constitutionality is now a permanent body with independent jurisdiction. Its purpose is to determine whether acts of the government or judicial system contradict the text or spirit of the document. Restated, this court will have the power to rule on the constitutionality of governmental acts. Such an extension of judicial powers implies an increased sensitivity of respect for constitutional procedures, as well as an attempt to strengthen Guatemala's legal mechanisms. Clearly, the key to success is dependent upon actual implementation; the verdict on the success of this novel approach to judicial review is still undetermined.

Congressional powers have been greatly expanded in two salient areas. First, the Congress will occupy a larger role in the formation of the judicial branch, and will in fact be responsible for appointments to the Supreme Court of Justice, the Court of Constitutionality, and the newly formed Human Rights Commission, among others. Additionally, members of Congress will also be able to serve in the president's cabinet without losing their congressional seat; such practices are ordinarily associated with parliamentarian systems. Accordingly, it was suggested that the new Guatemalan government would be of a semiparliamentary style.

Finally, with regard to the status of Belize, the new constitution suggests the potential for solving the question of Guatemala's claim of sovereignty over that nation. The executive branch is now empowered to attempt to resolve the situation, an issue that brings to the fore strong chauvinistic sentiment. However, any agreement must first pass through a public referendum before it can be finalized. The fact that the problem has been raised in the first place is, in and of itself, a significant element.

Overall, the new 302-article constitution is a detailed document—almost legislative in character. It raises, for example, a number of budgetary constraints on future governments through constitutional allocations of revenues toward major categories of national expenditures. Likewise, the political ramifications of the extensive attention to human/legal rights and its actual operationalization are a bit hazy in a nation whereby all accounts the judicial system and law enforcement are quite fragile. Yet the 1985 constitution was in broad terms a viable document and necessary for the successful extension of democracy in Guatemala.

The Supreme Electoral Tribunal

Formed in 1983, the Supreme Electoral Tribunal was composed of ten members, five of which served on a permanent basis and five alternates, who were capable of serving when a permanent member was unable. The members of the Supreme Electoral Tribunal were selected by the Supreme Court of Justice from a list of twenty names suggested by the Postulating Committee. During late spring 1985, the tribunal proposed laws that governed the November and December 1985 presidential elections; in turn, the executive branch approved those laws. Additionally, it was the responsibility of the electoral tribunal to supervise the actual electoral process. With regard to future elections in the post-1985 period, the Constituent Assembly also prepared applicable electoral laws.

8
The 1985 Elections

Introduction

In contemporary Latin American history, electoral campaigns have often been short on substance and reliant instead on party rhetoric and the charisma of the candidate. True to this tradition, the 1985 Guatemalan elections did not stray from this rule of thumb. For example, personal differences among the more conservative candidates oftentimes weighed heavier than differences in electoral platforms.

Overall, the breadth of representation in the Guatemalan political spectrum was perhaps the widest it had been in over twenty years—ranging from left-of-center to the extreme right (although numerically most of the parties fell to the right of center). As in the 1984 Constituent Assembly elections, any groups tied to the guerrilla umbrella organization, Unidad Revolucionaria Nacional Guatemalteca, were denied participation in the upcoming elections. As such, the extreme left was the only segment of the political spectrum that could not participate in the November 3 exercise.

Although coalitions changed during the electoral campaign, eight candidacies were officially announced. The following lists the parties, their presidential and vice-presidential candidates, and their position on the political spectrum, going roughly from the left to the extreme right:

1. *Partido Socialista Democratico (PSD)*: Mario Solorzano Martinez and Luis Zurita; left of center.
2. *Democracia Cristiana Guatemalteca (DCG)*: Vinicio Cerezo Arevalo and Roberto Carpio Nicolle; center-left.
3. *Union del Centro Nacional (UCN)*: Jorge Carpio Nicolle and Ramiro de Leon Carpio; center.
4. *Partido Nacionalista Renovador (PNR)*: Alejandro Maldonado Aguirre and Mauricio Quixtan; center-right.
5. The *Partido Democratico de Cooperacion Nacional (PDCN) and Partido Revolucionario (PR) Coalition:* Jorge Serrano Elias and Mario Fuentes Peruccini; right of center.
6. *Central Autentica Nacionalista (CAN)*: Mario David Garcia Velasquez and Carlos Molina Mencos; right.

7. The *Movimiento de Liberacion Nacional (MLN) and Partido Institucional Democratico (PID) Coalition:* Mario Sandoval Alarcon and Jaime Caceres Knox; extreme right.
8. The *Partido de Unificacion Anticomunista (PUA), Movimiento Emergente de Concordia (MEC), and Frente de Unidad Nacional Coalition (FUN)*: Leonel Sisniega Otero and Julio Benjamin Sultan; extreme right.

The Political Spectrum

Partido Socialista Democratico (PSD)

Having the distinction of being the only political party representing the ideological but democratic left in these elections, the PSD had only recently returned from three years of self-imposed exile in Costa Rica. (It did not participate in the 1984 Constituent Assembly elections.) Led by presidential candidate Mario Solorzano Martinez and vice-presidential candidate Luis Zurita, the PSD's participation in these elections was often overpublicized in an attempt to demonstrate the breadth of the Guatemalan political opening. The PSD is a member of Socialist International; Solorzano received the sanctioning of the latter through a public visit of support by the group's vice-president, Carlos Andres Perez of Venezuela.

Despite the PSD's recent revival in the Guatemalan political arena, the party confronted three major problems: (1) the party was divided into two feuding factions, (2) the availability of campaign funds was minimal, and (3) the right-wing labeled the party as communist, a stigma that frightened off potential supporters. In opposition to other political parties, the PSD's platform was viewed as quite radical, calling foremost for agrarian reform, among other substantial changes. In light of the party's internal and external problems, it was not considered a viable contender in the elections.

Democracia Cristiana Guatemalteca (DCG)

Led by presidential candidate Vinicio Cerezo Arevalo, the DCG was clearly a front runner in the elections. For many years the only traditional opposition party in Guatemala, the DCG had, to some degree, represented the entire left-wing portion of the political spectrum. However, since 1978, in the wake of an increasingly difficult domestic political environment, the DCG shifted to a more moderate image, moving to the center-left of the spectrum. This more moderate image attracted a larger constituency and, in fact, was attributed to the party's success in the 1984 Constituent Assembly elections.

In his early forties, Cerezo had been a party activist since his college days. Prior to the announcement of his candidacy, he had served as the DCG's secretary general. While short on governmental experience, Cerezo's charismatic personality attracted voter support. The DCG's vice-presidential candidate, Roberto Carpio Nicolle (related to the UCN's presidential candidate), while older than Cerezo, is also regarded as a pioneer of the party. Although lacking Cerezo's charisma, Carpio is an articulate politician, whose long-term association with the party gave the DCG's campaign an air of stability. In addition, with strong ties into the international Christian Democratic community (i.e., Venezuela and West Germany), the DCG received foreign financial and political support for its campaign.

As was the case with most of the other parties, the DCG ran much of its campaign on somewhat emotional rhetoric. The DCG foresaw the need to implement an austerity program to stabilize the economy, but specific outlines of this initiative remained somewhat nebulous. However, Cerezo's call for the country to unite behind such a program struck a harmonious chord in many Guatemalans. Emphasizing its anticommunist stance, the party centered its platform on its opposition to dictatorships of any ideological persuasion. Instead, a vision of a stable and democratic Guatemala under DCG leadership was strongly projected.

Union del Centro Nacional (UCN)

Founded just prior to the Constituent Assembly elections of July 1984, the UCN represented a new centrist political force in Guatemala. Its leader and presidential candidate, Jorge Carpio Nicolle, is a long-standing newspaper magnate. In fact, he used his publications (*El Grafico* and *La Tarde*) to carry out an effective media blitz campaign for the 1984 elections. His healthy second-place showing in these elections was directly attributed to the effectiveness of his media campaign.

A vote-strengthening three-party alliance with the Partido Nacional Renovador (PNR) and Partido Revolucionario (PR) collapsed in mid-1985, denting Carpio's election chances. Carpio's vice-presidential candidate, Ramiro de Leon Carpio, was a thoughtful and fairly articulate complement to the UCN ticket.Throughout most of the campaign season and subsequent electoral sequence, the UCN campaign remained in a strong second place, behind the DCG.

Carpio Nicolle stressed the concept of the UCN as the only valid center party in the Guatemalan political spectrum. Emphasizing that an economic recovery would insure political stabilization, his suggested policies captured an air of "supply-side" economics—at least in tone. Economic revitalization would occur through large increases in production levels spurred on by renegotiating the foreign debt, generating foreign exchange reserves, and creating a more favorable investment climate.

In the context of Guatemala's ongoing insurgency problem, the UCN argued that the creation of a democratic, centrist government should eliminate the insurgency problem; thus, the raison d'être of the Unidad Revolucionaria Nacional Guatemalteca (the guerrilla umbrella organization) would cease to exist. Should such an approach fail, it was widely believed Carpio would revert to a forceful counterinsurgency program.

Aside from the collapse of Carpio's three-party alliance, one other issue marred his vigorous campaign: the perception that his finances appeared to be of a virtually unlimited nature. And while obvious use of newspaper-related financial sources was made, the UCN refused to disclose its sources, a position similar to other parties. Consequently, wild rumors abounded as to the source of party wealth, which ran the gamut from the U.S. Central Intelligence Agency, to the Guatemalan armed forces, to a variety of domestic and foreign political and corporate sources. Despite widespread speculation, conclusive proof remained lacking.

Partido Nacionalista Renovador (PNR)

Led by presidential candidate Alejandro Maldonado Aguirre, the PNR is an older political force on the center-right, associated with Mario Castejon and other 1954 exliberationists. Maldonado had been active in Guatemalan politics for many years; in the 1982 presidential elections, he ran on the United National Opposition (UNO) ticket for president with Carpio (of the DCG) as his vice-presidential running mate. Widely viewed as a fraudulent exercise, with the "official" candidate General Guevara promoted as winner, Maldonado did claim victory in these elections. In the more recent 1984 Constituent Assembly elections, the PNR fared poorly.

Formerly part of the 1984 tripartite UCN–PNR–PR coalition formed in the Constituent Assembly, the PNR withdrew over a variety of technical issues, particularly power sharing. However, Maldonado did not appear to enlarge his constituency following his decision to leave the UCN coalition. Overall, Maldonado's image in the political spectrum was somewhat faded, being viewed as something of an opportunist, as a member over the years of a number of different political campaigns.

The PNR's vice-presidential candidate was a shrewd political choice, albeit an unusual figure. Mauricio Quixtan, who in 1984 made Guatemalan history as the first indigenous politician elected to office (in the Constituent Assembly), was somewhat surprisingly chosen as Maldonado's running mate. Quixtan's political appeal to the indigenous population stood in contrast to the PNR's conventional center-right constituency. Politically, the PNR's campaign strategy was of interest to the DCG, since it had the potential for diverting votes from the UCN on the first voting round of elections.

The Partido Democratico de Cooperacion Nacional (PDCN) and Partido Revolucionario (PR) Coalition

Formed in 1984, the PDCN was a virtually brand new political force in Guatemala. It sought Jorge Serrano Elias, ex-president of the Council of State under the Rios Montt regime, as its presidential candidate. During the electoral campaign, it was allied with the center-right Partido Revolucionario (PR), an older force in Guatemalan politics, which traces some of its roots to the October 1944 revolution that toppled General Jorge Ubico. But the PR is best remembered for sponsoring the victorious 1966 campaign of Julio Cesar Mendez Montenegro. The PDCN–PR's vice-presidential candidate, Mario Fuentes Peruccini was long active in the PR; in the 1970 elections, he campaigned as the PR's presidential candidate, only to be defeated by Col. Arana Osorio.

Serrano was viewed as having sound economic skills, generating support from Guatemala's entrepreneurial class. This was reflected in the PDCN platform or intended "plan of action" for the first ninety days of office: a strict austerity plan (i.e., reduce public sector expenditures, renegotiate the external debt, etc.) designed to stabilize the economy, and the beginning of a strong emphasis on weeding out corruption within the government. In the latter, one finds aspects that gained notoriety under the Rios Montt regime (1982–83). Serrano's campaign platform also drew from the PDCN's close grass-roots ties with the nation's cooperative movement. Of consequence has been Serrano's, and by extension the whole of the PDCN's, alliance with Guatemala's powerful and growing Protestant and evangelical movement. Serrano was the only non–Roman Catholic presidential candidate in a predominantly Catholic nation. Yet, the Protestant churches do represent in the upwards of 20 percent of the population, a fact that suggested a considerable potential bloc of support for the PDCN.

The PDCN did not participate in the Constituent Assembly elections, and therefore stood outside its 1984–85 deliberative process.

When the new constitution was issued in late spring 1985, Serrano was openly critical of it and attempted to distance himself from the document's perceived weaknesses. The party's "outsider" distinction gained it early support over the summer. But as the campaign intensified, the PDCN's growth—while representing a very potent political force—appeared to have slowed down; instead, Serrano remained a wild card in the elections.

Central Autentica Nacionalista (CAN)

A newer, conservative force in Guatemalan politics, the CAN was officially formed in 1974 from the roots of the Aranista committees that supported Col. Arana's successful electoral campaign in 1970. Formerly allied with the Movimiento de Liberacion Nacional (MLN) for the 1984 Constituent Assembly elections, the coalition earned the largest single bloc of representatives of any party or coalition. However, outside the MLN coalition, the CAN has limited organizational strength of its own; in the 1982 presidential elections it was reported to have garnered less than 10 percent of the vote, a trend that was to continue in the 1985 electoral exercise.

Leaving the MLN alliance in early 1985 for power-sharing reasons, the CAN announced its own presidential candidate, Mario David Garcia Velasquez, and Carlos Molina Mencos for vice-president. Director of the popular television news show, "Aqui el Mundo," Garcia widely utilized the television medium to launch his campaign. In addition to his journalistic talents, he was viewed as having sound economic capabilities.

The CAN (along with the MLN) has modernized its image and may be viewed as a "New Right." It has attempted to erase the political stigma attached to the older, conservative factions and has recruited younger blood into party ranks. The CAN's electoral platform reflected this neoconservatism: an intricate austerity program was called for, and the traditional values of liberty and the protection of individual rights were stressed.

The campaign was complicated by an unusual issue: Garcia's age. The Guatemalan constitution, scheduled to go into effect on January 14, 1986, with the inauguration of a civilian government, stipulates that the new president must be at least 40 years of age; Garcia was only 38. But despite the CAN's rejuvenated image, Garcia was not expected to finish in either of the two top slots on November 3.

The Movimiento de Liberacion Nacional (MLN) and Partido Institucional Democratico (PID) Coalition

The MLN is, at present, one of the oldest and most established political parties in Guatemala. Founded by Mario Sandoval Alarcon, who as patriarch of Guatemalan conservatism was its presidential candidate, the MLN traces its roots back to the 1954 "liberation." The party boasts a large constituency: in the 1982 presidential election, the MLN was reported to have garnered 25 percent of the vote; as indicated earlier, in the 1984 Constituent Assembly elections, it captured the largest bloc of seats. In contrast, the PID is a newer and smaller political party created in 1965 under the Peralta military government.

The current coalition (MLN–PID) was formed in early 1985 after the CAN withdrew from an alliance with the MLN. Both the MLN and PID were well-known for their hard-line, anticommunist stance, and, in general, highly conservative socioeconomic views. However, as part of the modernizing right-wing in Guatemalan politics, the coalition made concerted attempts to upgrade its harsh rhetoric, and courted new party members. The party's issues brain trust was made up of a comparatively youthful cadre of people.

The MLN's vice-presidential candidate, Jaime Caceres Knox, was a shrewd choice. Having little governernment-related experience—h_ was affiliated with the 1982 and 1984 Electoral Boards—Caceres Knox could not be linked to any earlier disasters at governance. An engineer and businessman by profession, he was a moderate spokesman for the MLN platform, with strong middle-class appeal. This was relevant to the extent that Sandoval is in ailing health, having a very limited public-speaking ability due to a tracheotomy. This obviously raised some questions regarding the actual governing capabilities of the MLN ticket, and placed further emphasis on the MLN's proposed government plan and vice-presidential spot in lieu of a physically impaired candidate.

The MLN remained a formidable force and was perceived likely to play a role in upcoming events. Its constituency was well defined, and organizationally undoubtedly ranked high. It ran in the first round, however, with a fairly crowded pack of conservative parties.

The Partido de Unificacion Anticomunista (PUA), Movimiento Emergente de Concordia (MEC), and Frente de Unidad Nacional (FUN) Coalition

Led by presidential candidate Leonel Sisniega Otero, PUA's ranks are, in part, filled by dissidents from the equally conservative Movimiento de Liberacion Nacional (MLN); in fact, Sisniega is a personal rival of the MLN's presidential candidate Mario Sandoval Alarcon. For the recent elections, PUA formed a conservative three-party alliance with the Movimiento Emergente de Concordia (MEC) and

Frente de Unidad Nacional (FUN). While FUN began as an informal political group in 1972 to support the frustrated candidacy of Peralta Azurdia, it became an official party following the 1978 elections. The MEC is an even smaller party, organized in the mid-1980s by supporters of Col. Francisco Gordillo Martinez, a member of the initial three-man junta following the March 1982 coup.

In the elections, none of the parties in the PUA–MEC–FUN coalition made much of an attempt to modernize their image and expand their constituency, as other conservative parties did. On a fairly narrow and traditional platform, the coalition espoused a virulent brand of anti-communism. None of these parties had a significant popular following; as such, even as a united force, the coalition was not viewed as a serious contender in the elections.

Election Day (November 3, 1985): Round I

Elections were held under generally cloudy, sometimes rainy weather, except in the coastal regions which fared somewhat better. Polls opened at 7:00 a.m. and closed at 6:00 p.m., with those standing in line at that time allowed to cast their ballots. Of the approximately 2.75 million registered voters, roughly 1.66 million actually voted, which translated into a participation rate of just under 70 percent. By comparison, approximately 72 percent of the eligible voters participated in the 1984 Constituent Assembly elections. Such percentages are higher than the traditionally low voter turnouts recorded in prior Guatemalan elections. Blank and soiled ballots, which had ranged at about 20 percent in 1984, were considerably lower this time (approximately 8 percent). This may have been due to better ballot marking procedures; the low percentage of blank ballots would also suggest that the political protest vote was kept to a minimum. It should be remembered that in these elections the electoral spectrum ranged from the extreme right to the democratic left, thus indicating marked expansion of the traditional range of legal political options in Guatemala.

Election day balloting proceeded in a peaceful fashion, with only a small police presence near voting areas. Registered voters went to the 5,142 voting tables (*mesas*) set up among the nation's 330 municipalities. There, individual voters presented their *cedula,* an identity card that indicated an eligible voter status. There were three separate colored ballots (white, blue, and yellow): the first for the presidential election, the second for the legislative elections, and a third for the municipal elections. A fairly elaborate and computerized system of voter registration lists, identity cards, trained voting table officials, watermarked security paper used for individual ballots, and the marking of individual voter's index finger with indelible ink not only appears to have precluded any organized fraud, but actually operated with considerable smoothness. It is also important to note that each political party could have representatives at the mesas to oversee the voting procedures. There were reports of confusion at individual polling areas, although in most cases it appeared to be random; in the majority of cases voters had simply approached an incorrect voting mesa. Overall, organized instances of fraud seem to have been frustrated.

Ballot counting began immediately after the polls closed. Hand-counted at each voting table under the supervision of both election officials and official party observers, results were centralized through municipal and departmental electoral boards and ultimately election headquarters in Guatemala City, at the Camino Real Hotel. After each mesa concluded its tabulation of votes, both election officials and party representatives signed an *acta,* which indicated the official vote count per mesa. Ultimately, the Supreme Electoral Tribunal (TSE) was to certify all the winners at the three levels of these elections. Most international observers were impressed by the integrity of the individual vote, the seriousness of the election officials, and the patience and good mood of the electorate.

Significantly, the presence of security forces was kept to an absolute minimum; in fact, in most cases, aside from local police presence, the armed forces were almost invisible. The latter, by design, were not allowed to participate in the elections. Likewise, subversive elements did not disrupt the electoral processes in any signficant way. There had been some concern that recent increases in guerrilla activity in the Peten region as well as in the provincial areas on the Pacific slopes of Guatemala's central highlands would limit voter turnout; however, this did not appear to be an element on November 3. Thus, neither physical intimidation from the armed forces nor from far left-wing elements was a factor in these elections.

Each of the three electoral contests operated under different vote-counting methods. An absolute majority was required to win the presidential/vice-presidential contest. As had been predicted earlier, a runoff between the two front runners was required and would be held on December 8. This second round of elections was limited to the presidential race. The other two contests (legislative and municipal) were decided by the November 3 exercise. In the case of the legislative elections that formed a new Congress, the winners were determined by a system of proportional representation, with each party drawing up a priority list of candidates. The municipal races utilized two separate systems: city council races used a system of proportional representation, while the mayors were elected on the basis of a simple plurality vote.

Results

Beginning with early returns the evening of election day, the Christian Democratic candidacy never lost its wide margin over all other seven presidential candidates. The DCG did well in its traditional areas of strength, primarily in Guatemala City and in other major urban areas. However, the DCG not only strengthened its hold in urban areas, but surprisingly won a majority in the traditional eastern strongholds of the MLN—El Progreso, Zacapa, and Jutiapa.

The race for second place had been viewed as a three-way race between Jorge Carpio of the UCN, Jorge Serrano of the PDCN–PR, and conceivably Mario Sandoval of the MLN–PID. The UCN came in a distant second spot with approximately 20 percent of the vote. Although clearly ahead of any of its other competitors, the PDCN–PR, which finished with approximately 13 percent of the vote, did not have as strong a showing as had been predicted. However, in considering that the PDCN actively entered the political arena less than a year earlier, its showing could be viewed as significant. As generally estimated, the MLN–PID coalition retained the support of much of its traditional constituency; despite its attempts to promote a modernized image, the coalition was unable to expand beyond that. It is also likely that the MLN–PID's campaign was hurt by the CAN, which finished in fifth place with just over 6 percent of the vote; it would appear that the CAN drew some of the conservative to moderate-conservative vote from the MLN–PID coalition.

According to the electoral laws governing these elections, Article 72 stipulates that any political party that garnered less than 4 percent of the valid presidential votes cast would lose its registration. This ruling affected the Partido Socialista Democratico, Partido Nacionalista Renovador, and the coalition of Partido de Unificacion Anticomunista–Movimiento Emergente Concordia–Frente Unido Nacional. A cancelled party registration as a result of these elections only implies that a party must reregister, which is a fairly straightforward task. Clearly, there was a psychological element here, particularly relevant to a party such as the PSD. Returning from years of self-imposed exile and representing the most leftist constituency in these elections, the registration issue and the low electoral support was something of a setback. For all parties coming in under 4 percent, there was also a financial issue in that they became ineligible to receive the government subsidy of two quetzals per vote. The latter is awarded every five years on the basis of valid presidential votes. For smaller parties, this financial aspect further compounds an already difficult political outlook.

Although overshadowed by the presidential race, the makeup of the new Congress was decided by the November 3 elections. Under the new constitution, the legislative branch of the government, at least on paper, acquired a new importance. On November 3, according to the electoral law, each voter was able to vote for different parties on each of the ballots, if so desired. Thus, the proportional party stength could differ between the presidential and congressional races, which in fact is what transpired. From available electoral vote counts, proportional party strength would vary greatly from that of the 1984 Constituent Assembly. The Christian Democrat presence in the new Congress would be roughly twice as large as that in the Constituent Assembly— holding fifty-one of one hundred seats. Of the more moderate parties, the UCN gained twenty-two seats, and the PDCN–PR gained eleven. The MLN–PID coalition would have approximately twelve seats, the PSD gained two, and both the CAN and PNR held only one seat. Results of the municipal races were less defined; final results were not released until late November.

The vote on November 3 set in motion the race for a direct and crucial confrontation for the presidency and the vice-presidency on December 8. This was to pit Vinicio Cerezo of the DCG against Jorge Carpio Nicolle of the UCN. Although Cerezo offered to integrate the UCN into his new government if the UCN would forfeit the second round, the UCN decided to see these elections through to their final conclusion. While the DCG was predicted by many to be the frontrunner on November 3, the DCG's overwhelming edge surprised many. In contrast, while the UCN had been considered a viable contender in the presidential elections, the party emerged from the first round in a considerably weakened position.

Election Day (December 8, 1985): Round II

Polls opened at 7:00 a.m. and closed at 6:00 p.m., with those standing in line at that time being allowed to cast their ballot. Approximately 65 percent of the eligible voters participated, down from 70 percent in the first round of the elections. The voter participation rate dropped off somewhat most likely because much of the population viewed the runoff election with a foregone conclusion; on the first round Cerezo finished with such an overwhelming lead over Carpio that most assumed the second round of elections would produce similar results. However, many observers were surprised that the turnout was actually not lower. As in the 1984 and 1985 electoral exercises, the military was excluded from all events; once again, only a small police presence was felt near most voting areas.

The voting procedures were identical to the successful November 3 format. A total of 5,142 mesas were set up among the nation's 330 municipalities. Each voter presented his cedula, which was then matched with a computer printout of registered voters. Before given a ballot, each voter was to sign his name next to where it appeared in the voter registry; once he had marked his ballot, the voter placed it in the ballot box, had his cedula stamped and returned (verifying his participation in the elections), and a finger was dipped into indelible ink to inhibit multiple voting.

Ballot counting began immediately after the final votes were cast and the polls closed. Ballots were hand-counted by the three members of the Supreme Electoral Tribunal (TSE) present at each mesa; the entire process was witnessed by party representatives seated at each voting table. After the tabulation of votes was completed, both election officials and party representatives signed an acta that indicated official vote counts per mesa. The TSE in Guatemala City coordinated the tabulation, and ultimately certified the vote count. Soon after the first results had been received on election night, it was apparent that the predicted DCG triumph was in fact becoming a reality. Jorge Carpio gallantly conceded defeat and Vinicio Cerezo claimed his victory.

By most electoral standards, and particularly by the tarnished practices in Guatemalan history, voting procedures were perceived by both participants and observers as almost exemplary. Much of the credit was attributed to the TSE and its president, Arturo Herbruger, and made possible by the organization's autonomous status, a situation not tampered with throughout Guatemala's 1984–85 spate of elections. The TSE's role, down to the individual voting table, was considerably upgraded through technical assistance from the Costa Rican–based Center for Assessment and Electoral Promotion (CAPEL), itself an arm of the Interamerican Institute for Human Rights. CAPEL also worked with the Center of Political Studies (CEDEP), a Guatemalan institution that provided training for polling officials.

The official role of the United States in the electoral process was, in spite of charges from critics, rather limited. The Agency for International Development (AID) provided $460,000; about half of this amount was used to purchase watermarked security paper for ballots and the balance of the amount was channeled through CAPEL for training. CAPEL trained 21,000 election workers that in the final analysis formed the backbone of the electoral process. Funds were also used to organize party poll watchers and assist in public education campaigns. With a less direct impact on election procedures, and involving more limited resources, the National Endowment for Democracy (NED) worked with CEDEP on polling and other public opinion activities. Yet, ultimately, the success of the entire electoral endeavor remains primarily a Guatemalan one. Without a certain amount of political will and a measure of prudence, the above resource input would have become a source of controversy rather than a constructive form of assistance.

9
The Transition to Democracy

Introduction

As theorists and practitioners alike often have to be reminded, democracy is never more than partially achieved. Even the countries of Western Europe and the United States, which have been at the forefront of this form of government, are themselves compromises, not the ideal, pure type. The latter is an abstraction and, therefore, like the greyhound chasing the wooden rabbit around the racetrack, a stimulating yet unattainable objective. Marxism, in contrast, is portrayed as a reality, in which lies both its appeal and basic weakness.

Such an illustration of democracy is not meant to impart the reader with a pessimistic impression of Guatemala's capability to institutionalize civilian, democratic rule. Instead, this is designed to serve as a reminder of the relative *reality* of democratic rule. Democratic rule in Guatemala and, by extension, the Third World will ultimately embody differing characteristics. The latter are a product of the nation's historical experience and culture. And while there are some key indicators that will appear in all democratic governments, the particulars will be quite different. Thus, in attempting to assess Guatemala's recent experience of transition to democratic rule, it would be inappropriate to measure the nation's experience solely against Western standards.

As with much of Central America, Guatemala has had little success with electoral politics, which is partially attributable to the lack of an institutionalized democratic party system. Political debates have resembled military ambushes, sparking an extraordinary degree of violence in the polity. Elections in the last four decades have been held on a regular basis but generally utilized fraudulent mechanisms. The 1984 and 1985 ballotting, however, began to suggest that elections could become an accepted mechanism for the transfer of political power and act as a consultative process between the population at large and the government. With that occurrence Guatemala was on the road to democracy.

The long-term viability of the Christian Democratic administration that took office in early 1986 is tied to a number of factors associated with the circumstances under which it came to power in the first place. As elsewhere in twentieth century political development, civil-military relationships are one such factor. To a large extent, the 1985 elections were a response to a legitimacy crisis experienced by the armed forces as the governing authority. Spurred on by this insecurity, the military focused intensely on the electoral process as the basis to restore legitimacy to Guatemalan governance—and, ultimately, to the armed forces as an institution. The 1984 Constituent Assembly ballot had already put a crucial aspect of the desired political order to test. In a more genuine form than previous electoral exercises, the 1984–85 sequence of events was clearly motivated by a desire for change. While the initiative was stage-managed by the military, it also reflected their acquiescence to possibly modify the nation's traditional modes of government.

The 1985 elections were the final stage in the withdrawal of the armed forces from direct governance and a concrete step in the formal transition to civilian rule. Some critics of the new Guatemalan government have charged, somewhat unfairly, that although there has been a constitutional shift, there has not been a substantial alteration in the composition of the power leadership. In this context, while the army has not abrogated its legitimate responsibilities, the concern for legitimacy that motivated the latter to pursue a form of regime transition suggests that the armed forces are willing to allow a modicum of free political competition and thus display their professed commitment to democratic government. In these matters, it is important to remember that new traditions are built over time.

The durability of democratic government is also likely to be dependent on the degree to which Guatemala's civilian political elites beyond the armed forces are willing to trust each other. As others have argued, Third World political development has been defined by a situation where mass political participation has been agreed upon among elite groups. In the Guatemalan case, while a semblance of consensus on this issue did develop, it was ultimately structured to restrict competition. The outcome of this "agreement" in the last several decades produced conflict and varying forms of suppression, the latter in lieu of mutually acceptable practices of competition.

In the present context, Vinicio Cerezo and his team face the delicate task of encouraging mass participation without either losing control of it or alternately provoking destabilizing challenges from opposition groups across the political spectrum. Beyond the established political formation, the government will also have to keep contending with the country's extralegal groups. Prominent in this sphere are the guerrilla factions, whose distaste for the current, fragile democratic order is well known. Also agonizingly difficult is the unpredictability of ethnic or Indian community cleavages and attendant politicization.

The ability of the government to address demands, respond to hopes, and thus appear distributionist in general terms is a third determinant of the nation's future political viability. Guatemala's difficult political circumstances are thus matched by a complex economic agenda that is at the mercy of social pressures in coming years and contigent on a carefully managed process of presidential and governmental promises. Vinicio Cerezo has only limited patronage to pass out, little of which is likely to make much difference to the electorate at large. A politically desirable approach, to a degree implied by the somewhat nebulous DCG electoral program, will be to attribute high levels of government achievements to a limited set of policy objectives. However, democratic electorates have fickle memories and can be very demanding. Like much of Latin America, Guatemala suffers from decades of misdirected notions of progress and prosperity, as well as the delicate balance between the individual and the state in this process.

Finally, the durability of Guatemala's new democracy also will be dependent on the shrewdness the current administration displays in the international sphere, and upon the opportunities this might provide. Obviously, fluctuations in the nation's external economic sector—much of it outside direct governmental policy reach—can have either favorable or adverse consequences for the government in the context assessed in the previous paragraph. But many Guatemalans will be looking for a more basic expectation ensuing from the international consequence of elections: the graduation of the nation to democratic status and personal economic well-being.

What will this in fact mean for Guatemala? The country could be rewarded in economic terms for providing the outward demonstrations of a political recovery. Furthermore, aside from these potentially material incentives, a democratic label could allow Guatemala to project itself more effectively in regional or international diplomacy. On the other hand, the more pluralistic political environment will also cause the government to be judicious in the articulation of its foreign policy activity.

The New Political Landscape

Having won an impressive electoral majority, the DCG started off with what can be viewed as a consensus mandate; Cerezo's presidential capabilities were enhanced by the fact that he was to work with a legislative majority and an overwhelming political base at the municipal level. Ironically, the DCG did not sweep Guatemala City itself. There, Alvaro Arzu, an opposition candidate for the mayoral slot of Guatemala City in the fraudulent 1982 elections, ran once again for the post. A charismatic politician, Arzu ran an effective independent campaign in the 1985 elections under the banner of the PAN. While the PAN is a separate political entity from all other parties, it did lean toward the DCG in terms of its political orientation.

The presidental runoff left Jorge Carpio and his party, the UCN, financially and politically exhausted. In the second round, Carpio's support came mostly from the capital city, and from Baja Verapaz and Jalapa. He was obviously not able to generate the conservative coalition some had hoped for, as the tone of the interelection period had suggested. Painting the DCG in often stark ideological terms that promoted fears of weak government and a left-wing menace, Carpio tried to resurrect a failing campaign. Never a traditional conservative political movement in its rhetoric, the UCN's nebulous "centrist" appeal and voter apprehensions relating to Jorge Carpio as a candidate most likely served as a salient factor in the unsuccessful electoral outcome.

With much of the Guatemalan party landscape centered around personalities, leadership predictably has become a critical variable. Many parties face internal personality challenges and periods of reflection regarding future strategy and ideological makeup. For example, Jorge Carpio of the UCN, Mario Sandoval of the MLN, and Jorge Serrano of the PDCN each represented much of what his individual party platform and subsequent electoral behavior was during the 1985 campaign. The electoral outcome continues to generate soul-searching and personality leadership changes.

In spite of the overwhelming DCG victory, its electoral opponents should not be discounted in the political battles Guatemala faces. Since January 1986, much activity has already occurred in the National Assembly and this suggests that direct party allegiances have instead given way to the formation of fluid power blocs. The UCN's working minority of twenty-two seats in the new Congress has already been affected by some defection. Likewise, the MLN and PDCN also have seats and local political representation with which to work, although in each (particularly the MLN) leadership issues have affected their previous vigorous character.

The overwhelming electoral victory of the DCG has represented a challenge. Understandably, the DCG wishes to retain its preponderant position and can do so by blending government bureaucracy and party structure. The temptation to institutionalize an electoral majority through various administrative reforms at the local and national levels is probably quite strong within the party's leadership. The challenge will be to build a democratic government without constructing an overbearing DCG dynasty. For the moment at least the DCG's internal divisions and Cerezo's overwhelming personal style seem to be two key factors worth watching.

Part of the outcome will depend in part on the diligence of the opposition parties. This is likely to include four diverse political factions: (1) the PSD, which continues to be the symbolic left-wing anchor of the nation's open political system, to which a rejuvenated PR could perhaps be added as parties operating on the DCG's left; (2) the Movimiento de Accion Solidaria (MAS), reconstructed around elements that have defected from the PDCN since the 1985 elections and headed by the still politically potent Jorge Serrano; (3) the UCN, whose ideological blandness and leadership squabbles remain major question marks, only partially compensated by a residual strength of its congressional representation; and (4) the MLN, the old conservative standard-bearer, but a party facing a profound leadership succession problem that is likely to affect its future existence. The smaller number of participants in the 1985 elections will remain essentially moribund until the next major contest; the PID and the CAN may ultimately be folded into coalition efforts, while the PNR will have to assess its de facto electoral alliance with the DCG.

All parties face a number of difficulties, perhaps the most important of which is learning to operate within the guidelines of what constitutes a loyal opposition party. Furthermore, with the next national elections not scheduled before 1990 (the electoral calendar also includes midterm municipal elections), it is difficult to predict what such a factor will have on the standing of opposition parties as well as their popular strengths. The viability of democracy in Guatemala revolves on the existence of a healthy competition between parties. This environment needs to be committed to alternative policy programs and there must be forces to play out the role of the loyal opposition, so critical to the Western notion of democracy. On a more practical level, the effective operation of political parties in the context of parliamentary deliberations rests, as it does most saliently in the U.S. Congress or European parliamentary commissions, on individual member and staffing capabilities, which exist in only minute supply.

With regard to Guatemala's executive branch leaders, the president and vice-president are both skilled veteran politicians. Their survival during the darkest years of repression of the more moderate portion of the political spectrum is a strong indicator of such capabilities. Appearing to be almost surprised by its own victory, the new goverment was slow to organize its new team. Having been on the defensive for so long and then required to govern and lead, the first few months of Vinicio Cerezo's leadership suggested an infant's wobbly walk. In fact, the new leadership appeared at first slow to form the new Cabinet and agree on the specifics of an economic program, only engaging with swift enthusiasm in Central America's never-ending "peace" process.

In his period as president-elect, Cerezo sped off to a running start. In the two weeks following his election, he traveled through Central America, briefly meeting with his counterparts in El Salvador, Honduras, Costa Rica, and Nicaragua. In addition, one and a half days were spent in Washington, meeting with members of Congress, the executive branch leadership, State Department officials, and several financial institutions. At various intervals, Cerezo grabbed the headlines. He mixed diplomatic realities with a dose of Guatemala's traditional sense of independence.

His first reception by Washington in his new capacity was warm, and generated greater public enthusiasm than Cerezo's "official" visit in May 1987. The congressional attitude seemed to suggest a positive direction for a probable American response to Guatemala's economic problems. The media's initial characterization of the nation's newly minted democratic government was hopeful and generally supportive. Obviously, events will be closely monitored by the international community; the Guatemalan experience could become a strengthening element in Central America's turbulent search for freedom, peace, and prosperity.

Vinicio Cerezo at the Helm

Vinicio Cerezo Arevalo of the Democracia Cristiana Guatemalteca was sworn into power on January 14, 1986. The swearing-in ceremonies were festive and well attended; Vice-president George Bush represented the United States. In historical perspective, Cerezo represented the first civilian president to occupy that office since the administration of Julio Cesar Mendez Montenegro in the 1960s.

Upon assuming office, the new government inherited a Guatemala plagued with problems: a prolonged and severe downturn in all leading economic indicators, as well as mounting inflation rates; the evaporation of foreign exchange reserves; continued political violence compounded by a latent insurgency; and, perhaps most damaging of all, a continued image in international public perceptions as a pariah state.

Guatemala's flawless November/December 1985 electoral sequence helped to neutralize the external political side of the above problem agenda. But the administration early on has received mixed views domestically; although a flurry of activity characterized the first few months in office, critics contend that little substantive progress was made on the major issues. Less charitable sources have suggested that the Christian Democrats have been unable to make the transition from an opposition party to a ruling force. To the extent that public opinion can be measured, Cerezo by now knows what it is like to be an incumbent.

Organizing the New Government

The implementation of policy was placed in the hands of a new cabinet, comprised predominantly of members of the DCG. This has included civilians who have participated in past governments, academics of a moderate political orientation, political bedfellows from the DCG party, and a few relative unknowns in Guatemala's political circles. Over a more than twelve-month period, some shifts in the cast of characters occurred, which as of summer 1987 stood as follows:

Agriculture: Rodolfo Estrada Hurtarte
Central Bank: Frederico Linares
Communications, Transportation and Public Works: Eduardo Goyzueta
Defense: General Hector Gramajo
Economics: Lizardo Sosa
Education: Eduardo Meyer Maldonado
Finance: Rodolfo Paiz Andrade
Foreign Relations: Alfonso Cabrera
Interior: Juan Jose Rodil Peralta
Labor: Catalina Soberanis
Mining and Energy: Roland Castillo Contoux
Presidency (political affairs): Sara Mishan
Public Health and Social Assistance: Carlos Armando Soto

In addition, the Cerezo government created two new ministries:

Culture and Sports: Anna Isabel Prera
Development: Rene de Leon Schlotter
Specific Affairs: vacant as of late 1987

The First Lady, Raquel Blandon de Cerezo, obtained a new and rather nebulously defined post of "special projects." Active in the political arena, Mrs. Cerezo has been reputed to have populist leanings that initially came to the surface during the early months of the government. This involved meddling in the government's touchy campesino/land rights problem area and demonstrating in front of the powerful business group CACIF's offices. This was rapidly toned down, but alludes to the internal divisions within the DCG family. Significantly, Raquel is not the only female figure in the National Palace; several young women occupy key "assistant" posts to the president.

A figure of note in the cabinet is Rene de Leon Schlotter, a veteran and founding political force of the DCG. Following the 1985 electoral sequence, he was rumored to receive the foreign ministry post (a rumor spread at his own behest). Backroom infighting between young and older, and moderate and ideological members of the DCG led to de Leon Schlotter receiving the newly created development ministry, a potentially powerful post if the DCG's electoral platform of regional development plans are ultimately suggestive of government policies. De Leon's first task has been to oversee the transfer of authority of the departmental interinstitutional coordinators and development poles from military to civilian hands. This ministry has had a delicate mission in which de Leon has been outflanked by other government institutions and the vice-president's office, the latter acquiring considerable administrative responsibilities.

Taking the lead on foreign affairs has been Cerezo himself, not the administration's first foreign minister, Mario Quinones Amezquita, who assumed control of the ministry as an unknown, both inside and outside Guatemala. Quinones has since been replaced (in late summer 1987) by the former minister of specific affairs, Alfonso Cabrera (the latter post remained vacant following Cabrera's departure). More influential has been the foreign minister of the outgoing military regime, Fernando Andrade Diaz-Duran, very much the architect of the framework from which Cerezo's foreign policy has been based. Andrade was in fact retained as Guatemala's chief spokesman at the United Nations.

More influential in Cerezo's cabinet has been the government's economic team, which has been built around the finance minister, Rodolfo Paiz Andrade, who comes from a successful business family (the Paiz chain of stores is the nation's largest). In this area of policy, the governor of the Central Bank and the economic minister have developed salient roles of technical and political importance.

Of other key posts outside the economic domain, the interior ministry's Juan Jose Rodil Peralta has occupied a sensitive position, being given the thankless task of both controlling domestic violence while cleaning up the nation's horrible record in this area. A new figure is Alfonso Cabrera, who was first brought in to manage the more recently created post of "specific affairs," a cabinet position designed to act in a backup and coordinating role to the presidency itself. As secretary general of the DCG and its moving force in the Congress during the 1986 session, Cabrera has also been viewed in some circles as a possible heir apparent. Confirming such speculation, Cabrera was moved to the foreign ministry post in the summer of 1987—a domain that Cerezo holds dear to his heart given the flurry of initiatives that have been undertaken since early 1986.

The defense ministry was originally put under the leadership of General Jaime Hernandez, at the time commander of the Honor Brigade. His appointment was viewed in Guatemalan circles as a rather innocuous one; close to the age of retirement, Hernandez was one of the least controversial military figures. His candidacy for the post apparently deflected the possibility for General Lobos Zamora, chief of staff under the Mejia Victores regime, to inherit the position. It was widely believed that the latter's appointment to the defense ministry post would have created strains for the new civilian government.

In late February 1987, a shakeup occurred within the ministry, triggered by Hernandez's retirement. He was replaced by the former chief of staff, General Hector Gramajo. Filling the vacancy in the chief of staff post proved troublesome. A potential candidate for the position, General Edilberto Letona Linares, was disqualified on the grounds of having entered into some rather difficult social relationships within Guatemala. In the spring of 1987, the post was filled by General Caceres Rojas, whose name has been mentioned briefly in connection with Washington's "Irangate" scandal. By early summer 1987, Caceres Rojas retired from the post of chief of staff and was replaced by General Manuel Antonio Callejas.

The Major Challenges

At the top of the agenda was the economy, which had been in a sharp tailspin since 1980. In early 1986, all leading economic indicators were down, and inflation was projected to be about 60 percent by year end. Of particular concern was the lack of foreign exchange reserves needed to pay for Guatemala's current import bill and service the external debt; in 1984, this stood at approximately U.S. $2.25 billion and, in 1985, due to increased short-term financing, it was approximately $2.5 billion.

Another issue facing the new government was the definition of the role of the military. The military had departed from office with a mixed scorecard. While it had been brutally effective in its prosecution of a counterinsurgency campaign, by most accounts it had fallen short in its handling of economic issues. Furthermore, their shepherding of the political process through 1985 had been notable, but, in contrast, it was widely believed that Vinicio Cerezo and his team would operate under a series of military-inspired political constraints. The new DCG government has appreciated this challenge fully, as have most politicians participating in the present political environment. The armed forces remains an important institution, at minimum by providing the support necessary for the new civilian government to function and rule effectively.

The role of the private sector was viewed as more problematic. The 1985 elections split that community, with the DCG's "progressive" economic and social rhetoric leaving portions of the business community nervous and unconvinced. A tacit working relationship was sought, and so far has successfully developed with the new leadership. Each needs the other, recognizing that the nation's future lies in a much improved economy. To assuage spirits, divisive concerns regarding major reforms of a social character have so far been left essentially unattended and do not appear on the horizon.

Compounding the government agenda has been its image in the international community. Vinicio Cerezo, who himself suffered, has come under severe international pressure to prove that the dark days in Guatemala's internal history are over. And in so doing, the international community has asked of Guatemala certain actions that could cause tensions domestically—particularly on the human rights front. The degree to which the civilian government has balanced its genuine commitment to human rights with both internal political realities and pressures from various international actors represents a major test of the nation's democratic institutions.

Guatemala's challenge from the left, in the form of guerrilla organizations, has not entirely subsided. Although the fraud-free vote, combined with the election of a moderate and socially conscious president, has placed the left politically on the defensive, the threat is far from gone. The approximately 2,000 or less active insurgents would remain a thorn in any government's side and have posed, in the Guatemalan case, a major political and philosophical challenge to the Christian Democratic government. Whether the issue is to be decided through talks, as vaguely proposed by each side, or through the pursuit of a counterinsurgency campaign—or both—could become an important barometer of the new government's policies. In the interim, leaders of the guerrilla organizations have remained skeptical that a civilian government will ever be able to come to grips with the nation's socioeconomic problems. Such skepticism may be hiding the temporary setback of the guerrilla cause, which, in fact, may be preparing the terrain for a possible campaign against democratically elected governments further down the road.

Overall, a first-year preliminary scorecard could look like this: civilian supremacy over the political affairs was reasserted; in tandem, the armed forces were moved to a position that can best be described as being on the fringes of the political arena; the private sector has played a salient role, but not directly, in the development of economic policy. Furthermore, far from beaten, although both politically and tactically weakened, the extreme left has reassessed its options in the context of the new political situation, potentially capitalizing on government indecisiveness or recurrences of violence. Clearly on the defensive and diminished in number, in 1986 insurgent-related violence was reported in at least eight of Guatemala's twenty-three departments. Potentially troublesome for the government's image is the cause of human rights, which has maintained itself as a politicized issue overseas, waiting to be used by a wide variety of critics at some opportune time.

Cerezo's task has therefore been far from simple. Elected with an overwhelming majority of the vote (69 percent), the administration's primary objective has been and will continue to be the institutionalization of democratic, civilian rule. Ultimately, the final evaluation of this administration's success will be twofold: (1) the ability to maintain and strengthen Guatemala's fragile political environment, while at the same time improving the nation's domestic economic conditions and international trade relations; and (2) to insure the orderly transition of power to another democratically elected civilian administration in 1991. In his search to accomplish these two objectives, Cerezo will have to practice the the politics of democratic prudence, combining pragmatism with firmness, and, in the final analysis, instilling domestic and international confidence in a rejuvenated Guatemala.

10
Democracy: Year 1

Introduction

The government of Vinicio Cerezo was elected on the premise that—unlike previous regimes—it was formally committed to improving the lot of the population. If the philosophical commitment to this objective appears quite sincere, translated into practice the reality is obviously far from simple. Although progress in economic development may be regarded as a necessary ingredient for democratic government, for the moment political stability may actually be the variable governing Guatemala's future. If the Cerezo administration can instill a degree of economic balance and political confidence in a somewhat traumatized society, a positive equilibrium will ultimately ensue. In fact, this very interplay between internal peace and economic growth will sustain democracy.

Guatemala's democratic hopes could be damaged by worsening socioeconomic conditions. After years of difficulties, voters went to the polls in 1985 less for the abstractions of political democracy than for the hope of improved per capita living standards. The inability to produce concrete results on this front would be harmful to the government; an actual or even perceived long-term decline of personal well-being would be devastating.

Cerezo's ability to consolidate his democratic rule will also be affected by the nation's external political environment. The latter imposes dangers, constraints, and opportunities. The government's projection of its own political ideals in foreign policy will be tempered by the reality that the domestic consensus in this area is shallow. Conversely, it has to take into account the very real dangers of external involvement in the delicate domestic political balance of Guatemala. Foreign and security policies will operate in tandem, implying a new and mature relationship between Guatemala's civilian executive and the nation's military establishment.

If a viable socioeconomic environment is indeed to play a role in establishing stable foundations for the democratic system, then the politics of international trade and financial issues represent major challenges. On a domestic level, the latter may test the Cerezo government's ability to bring together the nation's divergent views on economic matters. On an international level this could be made more problematic by any conditionality placed on foreign government credits and aid programs. The interplay of the U.S. Congress or European parliamentary commissions with Guatemalan politics has throughout the 1970s and early 1980s exhibited an unpleasant character. Thus, regardless of how painful this interaction may be to Guatemala's somewhat xenophobic instincts, in financial matters the nation will not build democracy on its own. How these external forces are played could very well assist or disrupt Guatemala's political process.

In meeting these challenges, the Cerezo government has initially done as well as individual assessment suggested he would; thus, some observers are hopeful, others frustrated. Writing in the summer of Cerezo's second year in power, one can note that he has stabilized the overall national situation, and many Guatemalans are grateful for that. At a minimum, he has added a more humane dimension to political life. But as the euphoria of the 1985 elections fades in the nation's memory, the real battle begins.

The Core Issues

After assuming office, the Cerezo administration channeled the majority of its energies into addressing four major issues: (1) stabilization of the economy, (2) gradual depoliticization of the military, (3) development of an activist foreign policy profile, and (4) attention to civil rights and legal procedures, police and security functions, and related human rights concerns. To American audiences Cerezo's foreign policy exploits have perhaps received more attention, whereas the interest of his national constituency has been obviously more stimulated by the government's domestic policies. Although this distinction obviously reflects legitimate American near-obsession with Central American security policy, the Guatemalan population's greater interest in socioeconomic matters underlines where practical priorities might ultimately be.

The Economy

Overall, Cerezo has been given a passing grade on economic policy. Nothing catastrophic has happened during the first year and, in fact, some economic vital signs appear on the upswing. Likewise, by moving slowly on socioeconomic policy, no constituency has been particularly hit hard; at the same time, few elements have been visibly affected in a positive manner. Significantly, the business community's confidence in government policies appears mixed at best, and the public's enthusiasm has been less than heartwarming. Still, by the middle of 1987 there appeared to be tentative signs of economic reactivation.

One of Cerezo's most pressing problems has been, and will continue to be, generating a renewed economic environment. Of all the Central American economies, Guatemala has perhaps the strongest base and shows the most potential for growth, despite a tailspin since the early 1980s. Years of insurgent activity and political violence led to massive capital flight, domestic recessionary trends, and corruptive waste in the governmental sector. This combined to produce for the incoming Cerezo administration an economically and psychologically depressed environment.

With this as a point of departure, the new government fumbled in its first year with an ambitious National Readjustment Plan covering all aspects of economic recovery: fiscal policy, public sector expenditure, monetary/credit policy, pricing policy, labor policy, salaries, exchange rates, international financial cooperation, and so-called immediate reactivation policies. The purported objective was to stabilize the economy and improve living standards.

These high-minded goals have brought few concrete results, although twelve or eighteen months may be too short a period for judgment. Even if the government can claim success for its stabilization program, it has been unclear what is to succeed it. The electoral promises for thousands of new jobs have naturally not materialized; in fact, reports are that unemployment (16 percent) and underemployment (46 percent) both rose in 1986. As expected, public expenditures grew, with a projected 1987 national budget of U.S. $950 million. Covered in part by foreign aid, government deficits likewise increased, but remain relatively low by regional standards. Yet, monetization of the economy is likely to occur if fiscal deficits become unrealistic; inflation went up to 33 percent in 1986. This activity stimulated some new momentum in the construction industries, ranging from roads to housing. With increased aggregate demand, Guatemala's Gross Domestic Product thus inched back to near-zero growth, but with demographic growth factored into it, it actually added up to about a 3 percent per capita GDP decline—for the sixth year in a row.

Mindful of political constraints, the government has cautiously decided to maneuver around the issue of agricultural reforms, regional development, and fiscal and monetary policy. Land reform, politically popular if an economically debatable item as elsewhere in Central America, has been gingerly approached.

Regional development, for which a new cabinet portfolio was created for Rene de Leon Schlotter, has the characteristics of a political fight in the making. Required by the 1985 constitution, the regionalization law has pitted the government against the armed forces, as well as the private sector's concern for bureaucratic and possibly wasteful government-led development projects. As well-intentioned initiatives to provide localized vigor to rural and some urban development, intended plans have, in part, run afoul of the army's traditionally catalytic role in this area. How regional socioeconomic development programs and the separate security function assigned to the army are likely to be reconciled does not have an easy answer. As a compromise, only the bare administrative outlines of a regionalization plan had been agreed to by early 1987.

Fiscal policy has been pursued on several different fronts, with government and private sector exchanges resembling a tug-of-war. The three-tiered exchange rate system, perceived as punishing Guatemalan exporters yet subsidizing imports was, for a period, a sore point with the private sector. Overall, the private sector has become nervous about mounting budget deficits and irritated by the government's method of upgrading tax collection. As voiced by the CACIF, the business community has tolerated but remains unpersuaded regarding the new system of export-import accountability.

At issue has been the work of the Swiss monitoring company, the Societe Generale de Surveillance (SGS), whose contract terms with the government were ultimately renegotiated in the summer of 1987. The modification of the SGS export-import control procedures was favorably viewed in the nontraditional sectors of the economy, where bureaucratic delays were correctly or incorrectly perceived to be the only impact of the government's monitoring efforts. The government, on the other hand, has claimed foreign exchange savings (through reviews of export-import transactions) of U.S. $30 million or more for the first five months of 1987.

The search for a stabilized socioeconomic picture has not been made simpler by the renewal of the trade union movement. Seriously impaired under preceding regimes, democratic politics have allowed unions to resurface—which they have done with caution. A certain amount of shifting and coalition-building among the principals (particularly the Confederacion General de Trabajadores de Guatemala—CGTG, the Confederacion de Unidad Sindical—CUSG, and the Union Sindical de Trabajadores Guatemaltecos—UNISTRAGUA) and industry unions (such as the Sindicato de Trabajadores de Industria Nacional de Electrificacion—STINDE) has already occurred, but no violent confrontations with the new government have been sought. Some unions' leftward ideological preferences will be as much of a political challenge to Vinicio Cerezo as the trade union movement's traditional foes in the private sector and the security services.

With a little luck and some help from Guatemala's newly found friends abroad, the external economic front has illicited some positive signs. Although this may be short-lived progress since the public sector deficit is likely to increase, the nation's external debt was actually reduced in 1986 (to $2.5 billion), keeping Guatemala toward the far lower-end of the scale in Latin America. Still, in 1986, 34 percent of the nation's export earnings went to pay the interest on the foreign debt.

Although current accounts have remained in deficit, the country was finally able to record a trade surplus. The nontraditional export sector, with some encouragement from the Caribbean Basin Initiative and the diversification of farm production, has begun taking on some importance. But several of Guatemala's principal traditional exports (sugar, cotton, and bananas) and nontraditional exports (oil, cardamom) were hit hard by nature, international market swings, and, in some cases, regulatory factors. For example, the tonnage allowed under the U.S. Sugar Quota declined from 82,000 tons in 1986 to 44,000 tons in 1987. On the positive side of the ledger, and offering a psychological lift, tourism rebounded during the first year of democracy due to the decline of violence and favorable publicity on the new government.

In the long run, the government's reactivation strategy of export diversification and promotion, and labor-intensive investment programs, will have to wrestle with growing and conflicting social pressures. For example, in May 1987, 200,000 public sector workers went out on strike. In September, CACIF and the government were exchanging serious threats over the implementation of a new tax package. And meanwhile, despite public sector investments, health, education, employment, and the thorny land-access question did not appear to improve much. Strategically, and perhaps correctly, the Cerezo administration appears to have placed political stabilization and economic growth ahead of traditional social priorities.

The Military

Cerezo's relationship with the military has been manageable, leading to the unfortunate implied criticism that he has therefore not succeeded in prevailing over army commanders. The basis of this new quid pro quo appears to involve acceptance of the military's preeminence in internal security and particularly insurgent matters, and the general isolation of senior officers from possible prosecution for activities undertaken under previous governments. In this context, the Mejia Victores regime's Amnesty Law remains key in this regard. On the other side of the coin, the military command's profound concern for Guatemala's previously tarnished image makes it a tactical ally in the protection of the nation's present democratic experience.

Prior to departing from office, the Mejia Victores regime undertook three actions whose effects have been and will continue to be felt in the Cerezo administration: (1) the 1986 national budget was approved, at that point by far the largest budget in Guatemalan history: 1,170 million quetzals (33 percent larger than the 1985 budget), with just over 50 percent of it devoted to three ministries—public finances, defense, and the interior; (2) a new method of calculation of import taxes, to be based on the quetzal value of imported articles, was put in place; and (3) an amnesty was extended to former members of the government and security forces linked to possible human right abuses committed after March 1982.

Since January 1986, the armed forces have played a background role, leaving Cerezo with considerable room to maneuver. But this is not to suggest that the military has surrendered all influence over events in the political arena—far from it. Cerezo's main challenge in this domain remains his ability to work with the armed forces on legitimate security issues (insurgency), while at the same time appearing firm and generating an image of independence from the army command on political and socioeconomic concerns. There can be no doubt that the president is conscious of this challenge, but it is unclear whether external or domestic critics are willing to see this situation in the same light and afford him the necessary time to create a new civil-military milieu.

At the same time a new milieu within the military itself was likely to be an issue of considerable interest during the first year or two of the Cerezo government. This became more evident at the beginning of 1987 when a shakeup in the military command brought to the surface fissures that remain likely to plague the armed forces through the projected elections of 1990. Careful political negotiations placed General Jaime Hernandez, an officer facing mandatory retirement within a year, as Cerezo's first defense minister. The two men who wanted the job, General Hector Alejandro Gramajo and General Rodolfo Lobos Zamora, waited in the wings. The former was named to the number two post (army chief of staff) while the latter was shipped off to Panama as ambassador.

From this arrangement, the first rotation took place in late January

1987 when the president named Gramajo as defense minister, effectively making him the person with which civilian elements must reckon
regarding military matters. A dynamic officer, Gramajo has been
regarded by some as relatively close to the Cerezo administration. And
yet, Gramajo has had several run-ins with the new administration; in
particular, both he and the minister of the interior, Rodil Peralta, have
met head-on over matters of internal security.

Despite these appearances of internal friction, the new defense
minister appears to represent a generally supportive posture toward
the new civilian government. In earlier years, Gramajo was sympathetic to the cause of the junior officers' discontent, which culminated
in the March 1982 coup. Having won high marks from his subordinates
for his performance in the highlands during the counterinsurgency
campaigns of the early 1980s, Gramajo has also been linked to the
democratic transition implemented by the Mejia Victores regime.

A former defense attaché to Washington, Gramajo has also attended
a number of U.S. army staff schools, including the Fort Leavenworth
Staff College. As a result, his reception by his American counterparts
during an official visit to the United States in September 1986 (while
still chief of staff) was warm. The atmosphere was suggestive of
improved bilateral military relations, which had soured and essentially
been broken off since the late 1970s.

Gramajo's nomination was followed by revealing miscues and an
expanding changeover of the army's major commands, leaving at the
time only two general-grade officers. The miscues were associated with
a certain amount of natural turbulence within the military ranks, which
in turn led to the nomination of two different chiefs of staff in a matter
of several weeks. The immediate outcome was the occupation of the
post by an officer, General Augusto Caceres Rojas, whose retirement
was to come in a matter of months. Caceres has been named by U.S.
press sources as a Guatemalan connection in the opening salvos of the
"Irangate" affair in Washington; the period in question was prior to
Cerezo's election. Although sympathies for the Nicaraguan external
opposition have probably been high in the military on philosophical
grounds, two Guatemalan governments in a row (one of them military)
have demonstrated a considerable reluctance to become involved in an
overt manner. In the interim, by early summer 1987, Caceres Rojas
retired from the chief of staff post and was replaced by General Manuel
Antonio Callejas.

Meanwhile, the military's handling of internal matters has not hit
any major crisis points. The 1986 insurgency campaign was a low-boil
affair, with left-wing elements shifting more to terrorist tactics and

attacks on outlying economic targets. However, the continuing threat has brought to the surface the army's equipment needs, which include rather basic requirements for ground and air mobility, such as spare parts and logistical and communications equipment. Limited U.S. military assistance (U.S. $5.3 million) was obtained in 1986 with slight increases possible in future years, conditional on congressional perspectives of Guatemalan political reforms. Although it remains a very potent force, the Guatemalan army has in recent years seen its neighbors turn into modern fighting machines, with spectacular Nicaraguan military developments as conspicuous as the growth and modernization of the Salvadoran and Honduran armies.

Foreign Policy

Vinicio Cerezo's foreign policy activity has been viewed by some domestic constituencies as a distraction from the real affairs of state. Designed to simultaneously isolate Guatemala from the region's geostrategic problems and yet place Cerezo at the center of the peace process designed to resolve those problems, the government has so far received mixed reviews and limited concrete dividends.

In attempting to find a position of noninvolvement between the pressures of the United States and latent threats of the Sandinista regime in Nicaragua, Cerezo's regional policy has only expanded upon the thrust of his military predecessor and his foreign minister, Fernando Andrade Diaz-Duran. But Cerezo's platform of active neutrality has been perceived by some as "neither fish nor fowl" or, worse, as suggestive of a potentially and needlessly unsympathetic attitude toward the United States. The latter is quite unlikely, but the perception—or its converse, sympathy for Central America's left-wing politics—has been enough to cause consternation among Guatemala's conservative and anticommunist elites. These groups carefully monitor the government's foreign policy orientation. Ironically, while much of the rest of the population is less interested with foreign policy issues, it is in fact this segment of Guatemalans that would support Cerezo's touch of national independence.

Observers of the Guatemalan environment suggest a very real strategic logic for the government's behavior toward regional issues. It is widely believed that Guatemala's insurgents have, for years, received material and logistical support from external groups. In an attempt to cut off these sources of external support, Guatemalan policy has shielded the government from political involvement in other regional insurgencies, and essentially suggested a hands-off approach toward neighboring governments. But Guatemala also runs the risk of becoming politically isolated if the plans for Central America's diplomatic leadership don't bear fruit soon. This leadership drive was seen in Cerezo's support to resurrect regional institutional capabilities (for example, the Central American Common Market) and efforts to create a dialogue through the formation of a regional parliament.

The five Central American presidents (Oscar Arias, Jose Azcona, Vinicio Cerezo, Napoleon Duarte, and Daniel Ortega) met in the Guatemalan border town of Esquipulas in May 1986 in a series of preliminary meetings to discuss the above ideas of regional coopera- tion. While all parties involved agreed in principle on a number of issues, such as the formation of a Central American Parliament, the meeting was not the diplomatic breakthrough feared by some and hoped for by Cerezo. Another meeting in Esquipulas was scheduled for the summer of 1987. Naturally, much of this diplomacy has impli- cations for U.S.–Central American relations and the future of peace in the region.

In this context, the first Latin American attempt to resolve Central America's conflictive environment via negotiations—the Contadora Group, comprised of the governments of Colombia, Mexico, Panama, and Venezuela—appeared to lose its way in 1986 and was replaced, first by a vacuum, and then by a Costa Rican proposal. In early 1987, the "Arias Peace Plan" was making the rounds of the relevant chan- celleries, satisfying or angering no one in particular. Although involv- ing somewhat different approaches to the resolution of the Central American crisis, it, like Contadora, left it up to Nicaragua to determine whether it could meet the democratic agenda being addressed by the rest of the region.

While seemingly endless rounds of negotiations failed to produce any concrete results, by mid-August 1987 the situation seemed to have reached a new turning point. The Reagan administration, in conjunc- tion with Speaker of the House Jim Wright, announced its own peace plan, only days prior to the second Central American meeting in Guatemala in early August. Such a move forced the hand of the Central American negotiating circuit, and the Arias Peace Plan was formally endorsed by the region's five presidents and reluctant acquiesence from the United States. However, by the end of the year, while tentative steps had been taken by the five signatories toward imple- menting the Plan, deadlines had not been met, suggesting a further lengthening of this "peace process." These meetings placed Guate- mala and its president briefly in the diplomatic limelight, although clearly the initiative shifted quickly from Washington to other Central American capitals.

However, the hero of the moment appears to have been the Costa Rican president, Oscar Arias, winner of the 1987 Nobel Peace Prize— and not Vinicio Cerezo, who was partially upstaged by Arias's efforts. On a domestic level, the implementation of this peace plan will require diplomacy at home. Although the Guatemalan military is satisfied with "active neutrality," it will remain so as long as the region's leftist threat appears neutralized by the policy. In contrast, other sectors of Guatemalan society have been more vocal in their criticism. The nongovernmental sector has reminded Cerezo in these trying economic times that Guatemala needs the United States. Certainly, much of the nation's political elite is philosophically and, to a limited degree, logistically associated with Nicaragua's anticommunist external opposition. Various sectors of Guatemalan society have become nervous by the prospect that if the reality of a Sandinista government becomes a permanent feature of Central America, Managua will become the political center of regional activity. What will happen to Guatemala in this context?

Part of the answer to that question lies in Guatemala's relations with an uncertain political environment in Washington. Relations have improved since Cerezo's election; the immediate result has been increases in foreign assistance, with 1987 economic and security aid levels standing at U.S. $149 million. While Guatemala has had a need for military assistance, this has been cautiously relegated to the back burner by both Guatemala City and Washington.

This is not to suggest that U.S.–Guatemalan security relations have been of no importance. In a crunch, in May 1987, the United States airlifted Guatemalan troops into the interior of the country. The use of American helicopters was politically significant in that it came one week before Cerezo's first official visit to Washington. The operation underlined the degree to which Guatemalan transport and quick-reaction capabilities were depleted.

Central American-related diplomacy and the Cerezo administration's regional initiatives have exerted strains on relations with Washington. In this context, Guatemala's policy of "active neutrality" and ensuing unwillingness to actively support U.S. policy efforts in the region have only served to complicate American policy. The promotion of alternative policies—such as the Arias Peace Plan and the creation of a Central American Parliament—have resulted in friction with the United States. Correctly or not, Washington has viewed these as dangerous vehicles, legitimizing ideologies, and even governments fundamentally unfriendly to Washington.

However, these considerations remain secondary to the strategic value of a democratic Guatemala. Washington has remained complimentary of the Cerezo administration's efforts overall and delighted by the process of democratization in Guatemala. For its part, the U.S. Congress has come to recognize this new reality and has, with residual expressions of concern, voted Guatemala varying levels of aid. But to cultivate this receptive environment in Washington, the Cerezo government initially appeared to fumble. For political reasons back home and diplomatic technicalities in Washington, the Guatemalan Embassy remained essentially unoccupied for a large portion of Cerezo's first year in office. This was ultimately corrected, not only by filling the Washington post, but by naming an influential vice-minister of foreign affairs, an old Washington hand, Francisco Villagran, to represent Guatemala at the Organization of American States, also in Washington.

As a significant counterweight to relations with Central America and the United States, Guatemala has engaged in a highly active and alternative diplomacy with Europe, and to a much more limited degree, Latin America. European diplomacy has been built on two bases: the Christian Democratic party connection, and the European Community's Central American initiative, which formally came to life in 1984 in the politically subtle form of economic diplomacy. A concrete expression of this was Cerezo's late 1986 trip to Europe with a large entourage of officials and friends. First stopping off in New Orleans and New York City (giving a speech at the United Nations), Cerezo met with Western Europe's democratic (Spain, France, EEC, West Germany, Italy) and spiritual (Vatican) leadership. Cerezo's visibility in Europe has served to counterbalance, with limited success, the Guatemalan left's considerable inroads there—which has provided the URNG with moral, political, and financial support.

This first presidential visit to Europe was well-received by Cerezo's sympathizers back home as a useful counterpoint to perceived American pressures. Although far from being enough to deal with the nation's economic problems, the trip reinforced earlier EEC commitments to Guatemalan democratic development—in and of itself an important consideration also of value to the United States. Aside from diplomatic support, a number of soft loans, government credits, and technical aid packages were put in the pipeline ($127 million in credits and $58 million from Cerezo's trip alone), along with a claim on the EEC's regional development budget. This cooperative environment was given a further boost in early 1987 when Guatemala hosted the third formal EEC–Central American meeting. By the fall of 1987, the European link, in this case Spain's socialist government, was being used as a go-between in preliminary talks (called for by the Arias Peace Plan) between the Cerezo government and its leftist guerrilla opponents.

The European initiative has overshadowed its Latin American counterpart, for good reasons, to the degree that the payoff in this area might remain symbolic for some time to come. Still, it has been important for Cerezo to rub shoulders with other democratic leaders in the region. Trips within the region, involvement in diplomatic peace initiatives, and the hosting of the Organization of American States' annual General Assembly meeting in Guatemala in November 1986 have been important psychological boosts to the nation's tarnished morale. In spring 1987, Cerezo played host to Miguel de la Madrid of Mexico, as well as the West German president, in a three-day highly publicized fiesta of warm rhetoric and painless agreements. Guatemala's acceptance as a respectable member of the international community was confirmed when its Third World peers voted U.N. Ambassador Fernando Andrade Diaz-Duran (until January 1986, chief architect of Guatemalan diplomacy) as president of the U.N. Group of 77 for 1987.

Entering the realm of Third World diplomacy may not be an easy task for Guatemala, but it might generate paybacks that may be set aside for future use. One such issue lies very close to home. The reestablishment of diplomatic relations with Great Britain in late 1986 was viewed by observers as the first step toward a practical assessment of the Belize question. Guatemala has retained its claim over that country, willing to break off relations with London in 1963 as British Honduras (now Belize) was granted self-government. Belize's independence in 1981 was never recognized by Guatemala, and remains an emotional issue.

Stiff nationalist sentiment has traditionally opposed any reconsideration of the question, which has forced Britain to garrison a 1,800-man force in Belize. A resolution of the matter could involve a face-saving "access" provision through Belize to the Caribbean Sea in exchange for recognition of the country's independence. Guatemalan economic interests might in the long run benefit more from this new situation than a maintenance of the status quo. But the territorial question is not likely to be viewed in this manner by Belmopan, where the issue is understandably a delicate one. Bilateral talks in early 1987, in and of itself a breakthrough, did not produce much immediate encouragement to Cerezo's sticky Central American sideshow.

Internal Order and Human Rights

When turning to the government's fourth major policy area, human rights, one penetrates a delicate policy issue. Vinicio Cerezo knows all too well both the character of the problem and the inherent limitations his administration operates under to address it. The situation has dramatically improved from several years ago, with the government now attempting to treat the malady rather than being one of its causes. Fortunately, the insurgency has been at a low ebb and army actions have therefore not been an issue. Efforts at addressing some of the roots of violence have been quite illusory; slowly, the country's police is being retrained and given new equipment, while attempts to upgrade the judiciary are being debated. The Grupo de Apoyo Mutuo (GAM) and the international community's human rights lobby remain a thorn in Cerezo's side, reminding his government of painful realities that continue to plague Guatemala.

One of these realities—the URNG guerrillas—has taken the shape of a marauding band of some 2,000 participants, operating principally near the Mexican border and in the Peten region. In the past, these elements have used Mexican territory and refugee camps as rear bases of operation, creating tension along the border. In 1986, due to diminished supply and membership levels, the guerrillas' tactic shifted to ambushes of soldiers and officers. Behind this lies the cat-and-mouse game that left-wing groups have been playing with Cerezo in which neither side has either the material or psychological momentum to launch any sort of direct assault resembling a "final offensive."

To overcome some of these challenges the Cerezo administration came in with hopes of addressing the nation's political violence through a multisectoral investigatory commission. In tandem, the government designed an anticorruption campaign. To deal with the government's own historically brutal record, Cerezo announced plans for new security measures, primarily geared toward upgrading the quality and expanding the size of the national police. The first major action taken by the new administration related to disbanding the dreaded Departamento de Investigaciones Tecnicas (DIT—secret police unit). As a critical adjunct to this, a restructuring of the nation's legal apparatus was recognized as a priority, yet movement on this issue has proceeded at a slow pace.

For all of this, Cerezo has received relatively good marks abroad. Indeed, from a distance, the overall character of tension and fear that had already begun to decline after 1984 has been further attenuated. It is obviously the *intent* of the Guatemalan government that has received the most attention—a major development unto itself. The governmental response to legitimate supply needs of law enforcement agencies has been relatively positive, with promises of material assistance for security equipment and some training from West Germany and several other nations. The psychological break with Guatemala's violent past permitted the Reagan administration in 1986 to make the case for certification of progress on human rights and political conditions before the U.S. Congress. The same year, the OAS Human Rights Commission noted in its annual review that the situation in Guatemala had changed measurably. By early 1987, the United Nations Human Rights Commission had also begun to revise its critique of the Guatemalan situation primarily on the basis of a restoration of hope.

Others have focused on the specific reality, which while greatly improved remains appalling in some aspects. Without the realization that politically motivated deaths (by U.S. Embassy reports) in 1981 numbered about 350 per month, does the figure of about six per month in early 1986 reflect any real progress? In other words, the mere fact that low-level violence has continued would seem to suggest that a complete rejuvenation has not occurred. When announcing the government's new security and police training measures in June 1986, Interior Minister Juan Jose Rodil Peralta was quoted as stating that generalized violence had claimed the lives of more than 700 people since Cerezo's inauguration in January. Although the guerrillas must clearly take responsibility for much of the national violence, the country's conservative elements have also contributed a significant element in this regard; renegade elements of the security forces are also not above suspicion.

To make the government's position more difficult, most international human rights organizations (Americas Watch and Amnesty International, for example) have withheld giving Guatemala an approval rating, except to suggest that the government was now at least trying to ameliorate domestic conditions. This has affected the response of the parliamentary bodies of Western Europe (particularly in northern Europe) and the United States when asked to vote for aid to Guatemala. However, the early 1987 attack on a lawyer associated with Amnesty International's efforts to open an office in Guatemala only seemed to confirm the critics' suspicions.

Cerezo's electoral commitment for an investigatory commission on past human rights abuses has continued to haunt the government. The issue initially had some chance of disappearing from the priority agenda due to a sympathetic response for Cerezo's overall efforts, but has been kept in the limelight by GAM. This group has dogged the Guatemalan government since 1985, and has represented an uncomfortable problem for Cerezo after assuming the presidency. In this context, he has maneuvered around GAM by first suggesting that the Supreme Court, not the planned commission, would investigate GAM's list of 1,467 disappearances. Under continued pestering from GAM, in late 1986 Cerezo agreed to create some form of investigatory commission. But unequivocally, he also excluded the military's past record from consideration.

Another tenacious problem has been the never-ending insurgency, itself the cause of the human ravages of the late 1970s and early 1980s. In prosecuting the war, the new democratic government faces profound dilemmas. Unless the guerrillas are beaten or bought back to the fold, the government program to combat violence—and for that matter, its entire political program—will come to naught. Guatemalan army sources placed active URNG supporters at about the 6,000 level, in addition to 2,000 armed guerrillas. The level of confrontation in 1987 seemed to suggest that despite past efforts, a network of informers and supplies still existed in the highland regions of the country.

To fight, the government needs the armed forces, but this institution remains suspicious of any overture by the government toward the left. Under the looking glass of international human rights organizations, or GAM and the Guatemalan Human Rights Commission, Cerezo cannot afford any sloppy mistakes on the part of the armed forces or the security police. But if he does not act forcefully, the left is likely to attempt to take his democratic government down toward destruction.

Uncertain of its prey, the URNG has cautiously recognized that its depleted manpower, lack of public goodwill, and the relative popularity of Vinicio Cerezo might suggest a policy of tempting the government into some form of political dialogue. Over a one-year period (1986–87) the guerrillas allegedly tried three times with varying forms of conditions, and then proposals. With the deeply Marxist and authoritarian character of the URNG, none of these suggestions were likely to appeal to the government, and even less to the armed forces. In fact, the very legitimacy of the violent left appeared in question in the face of Vinicio Cerezo's democratic credentials. Thus, Cerezo's return volley—suggesting that a talk might be possible if the guerillas laid down their arms—fell on deaf ears, since without weapons the URNG appeared to be a politically impotent force for the time being. Would this be temporary? A partial answer was to be given in the context of Central American "peace" negotiations, when in the fall of 1987 the government and the guerrillas officially met (in Spain) to discuss an uncertain agenda.

Conclusion

When analyzing their own circumstances, Guatemala's Christian Democratic political leaders were most likely surprised by the extent of the 1985 electoral triumph. To a degree, they were unprepared to

govern and physically decimated during the previous military government tenure. It is therefore quite extraordinary that democratic governance took hold of the institutional framework on January 14, 1986. To
the critics' surprise, most constituencies—including the military—
acquitted themselves well in this transition process. The subsequent
experience suggests a Guatemala gingerly moving forward to tackle its
serious political and economic agenda.

To provide a realistic portrait of the Guatemalan political puzzle,
and a sense of its constraints, it would be misleading to imply from the
above assessment that new political traditions are now firmly rooted.
In fact, as some analysts of Latin American democratization have
suggested, Guatemala is in a remissive or predemocracy stage. As
frustrating as this concluding assessment might be for those involved
in Guatemala's democratic experience, it is better to admit the fragility
of this experience than to overestimate the actual strength of the new
form of governance. This is relevant for both the American and the
Guatemalan readers of this book; one can identify several points in
this regard.

In suggesting a remissive democracy, the authors are approximating
the situation as it exists—as opposed to an idealistic vision of a
democratic Guatemala. From this flows two salient policy implications.
First, although the civilian government of Guatemala is very conscious
of its limitations, elements surrounding it on both a domestic and
international level may not be that realistic. By dealing with the nascent
character of the democratic process, the policy community in Guatemala and elsewhere can provide responses that match the political
conditions. If, instead, unrealistic expectations govern actions, the
nation's delicate political process is not likely to build secure foundations. Second, realistically dealing with the fragile environment can
diminish the disappointments if the process wavers somewhat. Alternatively, a practical assessment of the situation is most likely to add a
sense of real accomplishment when, in the future, democracy becomes
firmly rooted.

If not attentive to these considerations, Guatemala's delicate political reconstruction could be undermined by actions or inactions of the
United States and European nations. To a degree, the greatest challenge to Guatemala lies in its ability to overcome the reticence of the
international democratic community to respond at all. Alternatively,
the latter's actions can invigorate the process of democratization by
providing a helping hand. This is not to be envisioned as "creating"
democracy in Guatemala for only Guatemalans can do that; but if the

seeds are there, and they are, then the Western democratic community can play a constructive and timely role.

Ultimately, Guatemalan democracy needs to simultaneously address the challenges of economic development with some degree of social equality, while proceeding ahead with a strengthening of the nation's political development institutions. This is a difficult mix for any nation to both plan and address. Vinicio Cerezo cannot be compared to either Abraham Lincoln or Jose Marti in that he most likely does not represent a powerful philosophical foundation of a nation in distress. Fortunately, despite Latin American Christian Democracy's occasional proclivity to swing across the political spectrum in a radical fashion, Cerezo cannot be compared to Fidel Castro. What the leadership elected in late 1985 does represent is a commitment to democratic government. Obviously, that may not be enough.

Placing theory aside, democratic government requires a concern for societal mobility; it requires a deepening of the concept of loyal political opposition; it requires attention to detail rather than a fascination with grand concepts—Guatemala's political and economic stabilization and, ultimately, the development process, is like a modern business and has to be run in an efficient manner. In the final analysis, Guatemalan democracy demands loyalty to a constitutional government. Segments of the current array of forces within Guatemala and in Central America as a whole do not yet conceive of their future in these exact terms. But the 1986 democratic opening suggests a positive evolutionary solution to Guatemala's political puzzle.

Bibliographic Note

The opening line of a 40-year-old French novel, later made into a film, may suggest an exaggerated image of this Central American nation: "Guatemala doesn't exist; I know, I've been there" (Georges Arnaud, *Le Salaire de la Peur*). In fact, a great deal of the information about Guatemala available to foreigners is second-hand and second-rate. One might go further and suggest that the relevant political literature is not only weak, but in many areas of analysis, thin. As a result, Guatemala is forever at the mercy of an itinerant columnist or critic who, after lunch at the Camino Real Hotel or a trip to a refugee camp, is ready to pronounce him or herself upon the fate of the Guatemalan people.

Realism is generally considered necessary in the effort to make the study of politics serious, if not scientific. But when writers have turned to the study of Guatemala, most have tended to implicity acknowledge that realism had no place, and was to be substituted for a dose of emotional sentiment. This is reflected in many of the popular and specialized literature generated over the years bearing such imaginative titling as: *Dare to Struggle, Dare to Win*; *Death before Breakfast*; *Garrison Guatemala*; *Little Hope*; "The Muffled Scream"; "Tropic of Fire"; *Tyranny on Trial*; *Unnatural Disaster*; *Witness to Genocide*; *The Shark and the Sardines*; and *Bitter Fruit*, the latter two titles of minor bestsellers on the 1954 episode and related matters. This suggests that a treatise on most aspects of Guatemalan life has become more of an exercise in constructing self-interested manipulations of the nation's political affairs than an empirical assessment of political dynamics. No doubt, soon to become a classic of this genre is Jean-Marie Simon's *Guatemala: Eternal Spring, Eternal Tyranny* (1987), which skillfully combines highly emotional photography with a heavily–biased political analysis to produce a volume essentially dedicated to the discrediting of the nation's preliminary democratic experience.

Admittedly, Guatemala's recent history of crisis and violence has been a boon to quick and dirty accounts. Thus, certain issues and periods have been picked over with considerable fervor, if not always respectable scholarship. The 1954 revolution and Guatemala's frequent bouts with instability have, legitimately, received much attention. But

113

the English-speaking (and perhaps even Spanish-speaking) reader hungering for more complete assessments of Guatemalan sociopolitical development soon finds him or herself on very short rations.

This is not to suggest that there is nothing to read on Guatemala. On the contrary, a bibliography prepared in conjunction with the present study produced a document sixty-nine pages long—which did not even involve a deep search of non-English language titles.

The nation's rich ethnology has generated a literature of quality, with extensions into Guatemala's archeological and colonial past. No observer of Guatemalan affairs can afford to omit spending a few hours reviewing the Mayan-Toltec civilizations that preceded the Spanish conquest and still constitute a fundamental feature of modern Guatemala. If a trip to Guatemala, highly recommended as it is the most striking nation in the region geographically and culturally, is not feasible, consult a general history of the Mayan culture such as *The Ancient Maya* (1983), by Morley, Brainerd, and Sharer, or in a broader vein, *Sons of the Shaking Earth* (1959) by Eric Wolf. Also of interest is the modern and somewhat politically suggestive cultural study by Jean-Christian Spahni, *Los Indios de America Central* (1981). A more specialized volume is that of Robert Carmack, *The Quiche Mayas of Utatlan* (1981). For an entertaining, if somewhat politicized, view of the modern Indian community and life, James D. Sexton's two companion diaries are interesting: *Son of Tecun Uman* (1981) and *Campesino* (1985). The various works by the Melvilles are also useful in this context. A general work on Guatemala's transition to and experience during the colonial period is the highly readable *Spanish Central America* (1973) by Murdo MacLeod. And for a pictorial view of the nation about 100 years ago, the beautifully produced volume of photographs as a social recorder, *Eadward Muybridge in Guatemala, 1875* (1986) by E. Bradford Burns, is a must.

Although Guatemala has sustained a strong cultural environment, particularly in the visual arts, as in the rest of Central America, it has not produced a literary tradition of any international distinction. Among a few notable exceptions is Nobel Prize winner Miguel Angel Asturias. His *El Senor Presidente* is a novel built around a caricature of authoritarian figures of the nineteenth and early twentieth century period and particularly the long Estrada Cabrera tenure (1898–1920). (As a side note: Asturias's son has become one of the major leaders of the Marxist guerrillas fighting successive Guatemalan governments.)

Guatemala's first century of independence through World War II remains partially studied, primarily through monographic studies. One among several interesting vignettes in English is provided by D.J.

McCreery, in *Development and the State in Reforma Guatemala* (1983), which deals with the 1870–80 period under President Barrios. Covering a recent and important period, that of Jorge Ubico (1931–44), is the thoroughly researched analysis by Kenneth J. Grieb, *Guatemalan Caudillo* (1979).

The literature on modern Guatemala fills many pages. Part of this output continues to be concentrated around anthropological interests. Some of the latter is of a scholarly character, but contemporary political analyses have little such theoretical pretention. A great deal of it is, in fact, politically motivated, and centered around two overlapping grand themes: (1) the 1944–54 political experience and an assessment of the American role in it, and (2) the salience of violence and inequality in Guatemalan society (particularly since the 1960s) and the perceived American responsibility in its maintenance. This is a minefield for the uninitiatied reader, as it includes outright trash, political tracks masquerading as scholarship, a number of task-force or commission-type special interest reports, and a limited amount of sophisticated work on politics and economics. To this, one needs to add the output of the popular press, including newsletters and magazines, and also journal articles.

The 1944–54 period has tended to be the beginning (and at times the end) of a lot of what has been written on Guatemala of a political vein. For many writers it is the anchor to which a glorious but aborted potential of national development is attached, and from which the basis for an explanation of the subsequent trials and tribulation of Guatemalan society is derived. The period has generated polemical defenses and attacks, but the definitive analytical works have yet to be written. The American reader will want to take a look, with all of its imperfections, at Ronald Schneider's *Communism in Guatemala, 1944–54* (1958), on the one hand, and *Bitter Fruit* (1982) by Schlesinger and Kinzer, on the other. For those with Nicaragua and other Central American issues on their mind, Schneider's twenty-year-old analysis is quite revealing. In a broader sociological vein, R.N. Adams's minor classic, *Crucifixion by Power* (1970), is also of interest.

A review of the English and Spanish-language titles published in an American academic journal suggest the pitfalls of the literature on developments since the 1960s (see Forrest D. Colburn, "De Guatemala a Guatepeor," *Latin American Research Review* 21, No. 3 [1986]). The review contains two volumes bordering on the diatribe that have been widely available in American bookstores: *Guatemala in Rebellion: Unfinished History* (1983) edited by Fried, Gettleman, Levenson, and Peckenham, and *Garrison Guatemala* (1984) by George Black and two associates. Colburn's mildly sympathetic book review does note that the personal convictions and political persuasions of the authors are widely apparent; of interest, he correctly notes the near absence of articulate, alternative views of Guatemala's experience. (The Bouchey and Piedra volume, *Guatemala: A Promise in Peril* [1980], is very dated and incomplete.)

Another widely distributed book (not reviewed by Colburn) is Michael McClintock's *The American Connection: State Terror and Popular Resistance in Guatemala* (1985). It contains an informative bibliographical research note. This is an artfully researched volume by an Amnesty International staffer who, if the reader is not on his guard, does a masterful job of linking Guatemala's unhappy political experiences with U.S. policy. This feeds on the widely held view of the purported strategic interest of the United States to keep the region in the Stone Age. Such a linkage confuses the resistance toward modernization of segments of Guatemalan elites with the ultimate inattention for Central American problems by succeeding American administrations. Older works, such as Daniel James's *Red Design for the Americas: Guatemalan Prelude* (1954), have, with their archaic notions of global strategic relationships and local political development done much to sustain the above view of American policy in the region.

A sample of focused works on the military and Guatemala's political dynamics includes studies by Cesar D. Sereseres (at his best when discussing Guatemala's military) and several of his associates at the Rand Corporation (Luigi Einaudi, Brian Jenkins). Piero Gleijeses is a good source for a very sympathetic view of Guatemala's far left. A contrast of the above authors is found in the School for Advanced International Studies's *Report on Guatemala* (1985). For a detailed analysis of Guatemala's 1985 political transition and electoral politics see Georges Fauriol and Eva Loser, *Guatemalan Election Study Report* (1986).

A number of specialized publications have in recent years focused specific attention on Guatemalan affairs. Many of these emanate from American or European human rights and religiously affiliated organizations (Washington Office on Latin American—WOLA, or Americas Watch Committee, for example), and also from highly politicized groups (mainly on the liberal left), such as the EPICA Task Force and the North American Congress on Latin America (NACLA). The reports emanating from Amnesty International and the International Commission of Jurists are widely read (and quoted) and are interesting to contrast with those of the U.S. Department of State.

For outsiders looking in, *Central American Report* is a useful weekly newsletter published in Guatemala that, while not fully reliable, is at least consistent. The parent organization, Inforpress Guatemala, also issues a number of specialized publications. There is an active if less than reliable printed media in Guatemala; in any event, little of it is available in the United States. *Cronica,* a newsweekly that began publication in 1987, held promise of a more vigorous quality press. As for the American press, much of its coverage of Guatemala has been episodic and somewhat sensational. In recent years, the *New York Times*, the *Washington Post*, the *Los Angeles Times*, and, selectively, the *Wall Street Journal*, the *Miami Herald*, and the *Christian Science Monitor* have provided a limited selection of stories.

Among several Guatemalan research organizations, the Centro de Investigaciones Economicos Nacionales (CIEN) has in recent years published useful politico-economic reports. The foundation FADES' (Fundacion para el Analisis y el Desarrollo de Centroamerica) weekly newsletters, *Analisis Politico* and *Analisis Economico,* provide well-informed assessments of national and regional developments. Guatemala's private sector (through CACIF or the Chamber of Commerce) has over the years published its own visions of the nation, some more noteworthy than others. The *Analises de la Situacion Economica de Guatemala, 1965–1984* (1984) is one of its more worthy efforts. With an eye to the American market, new publications such as *Viva Guatemala!* (with a trial issue appearing in 1986 published by FUNDESA—a private sector foundation) have attempted to reshape the tainted image of Guatemala overseas.

Placing Guatemala in its modern Central American context is most effectively done by Ralph Lee Woodward is *Central America* (2nd ed., 1985), a straightforward and very readable up-to-date history. Guatemala is well covered in the annotated bibliography (pp. 308–61), which is well worth the price of this paperback edition. There are few comprehensive historical treatments of Guatemala; *The Gift of the Devil* (1984) by Jim Handy is a well-researched if somewhat politically oriented attempt. Peter Calvert's *Guatemala: A Nation in Turmoil* (1985) is a more comprehensive, but uneven, volume.

The above is a review of selected titles. The bibliography below includes the titles reviewed here. This is not an exhaustive reading list but it does include titles geared toward the subject matter treated in this book and toward the English-speaking reader in particular.

Adams, Richard Newbold. *Crucifixion by Power: Essays on Guatemalan National Social Structure, 1944–1966.* Austin, Texas: University of Texas Press, 1970.
Aguilar Zinser, Adolfo. "Mexico and the Guatemalan Crises." In *The Future of Central America: Policy Choices for the U.S. and Mexico,* edited by Richard R. Fagen and Olga Pellicer. Stanford, Calif.: Stanford University Press, 1983.
Aguilera, Gabriel. "The Massacre at Panzos and Capitalist Development in

Guatemala." In *Revolution in Central America*, edited by Stanford Central America Action Network. Boulder, Colo.: Westview Press, 1983.

Albizurez, Miguel Angel. "Struggles and Experiences of the Guatemalan Trade Union Movement, 1976–June 1978." *Latin American Perspectives* 7 (Spring–Summer 1980).

American Association for the International Commission of Jurists. *Guatemala: A New Beginning*. New York: American Association for the International Commission of Jurists, 1987.

Americas Watch. *Human Rights in Guatemala: No Neutrals Allowed*. New York: Americas Watch Committee, 1982.

———. *Guatemala: A Nation of Prisoners*. New York: Americas Watch Committee, 1984.

———. *Little Hope: Human Rights in Guatemala, January 1984 to January 1985*. New York: Americas Watch Committee, 1985.

Amnesty International. *Guatemala: A Government Program of Political Murder*. London: Amnesty International Publications, 1981.

Amurrio, Jesus J. *El Positivismo en Guatemala*. Guatemala: Editorial Universitaria, 1966.

Asturias, Miguel Angel. *Guatemalan Sociology*. Tempe, Ariz.: Arizona State University, Center for Latin American Studies, 1977.

Asturias, Miguel Angel. *El Senor Presidente*. Paris: Editions Klincksieck, 1978 (edicion critica).

Aybar de Soto, Jose M. *Dependency and Intervention*. Boulder, Colo.: Westview Press, 1978.

Barber, Willard F., and C. Neale Ronning. *Internal Security and Military Power: Counterinsurgency and Civic Action in Latin America*. Columbus, Ohio: Ohio State University Press, 1966.

Barry, Tom. *Guatemala: The Politics of Counterinsurgency*. Albuquerque, N.M.: The Inter-Hemispheric Education Resource Center, 1986.

Berryman, Phillip. *The Religious Roots of Rebellion: Christians in Central American Revolutions*. Maryknoll, N.Y.: Orbis Books, 1984a.

———. *Christians in Guatemala's Struggle*. London: Catholic Institute for International Relations, 1984b.

Bicudo, Helio Periera. *Mi Informe Sobre El Escuadron de la Muerte*. Madrid: Ultramar Editors, SA, 1978.

Black, George. *Garrison Guatemala*. New York: Monthly Review Press, 1984.

Blaufarb, Douglas S. *The Counterinsurgency Era: U.S. Doctrine and Performance, 1950 to the Present*. New York: Free Press, 1977.

Bouchey, L. Francis, and Alberto M. Piedra. *Guatemala: A Promise in Peril*. Washington, D.C.: Council for Inter-American Security, 1980.

Bowen, Gordon L. "U.S. Foreign Policy Toward Radical Change: Covert Operations in Guatemala, 1950–1954." *Latin American Perspectives* 10 (Winter 1983).

———. "U.S. Policy Toward Guatemala, 1954 to 1963." *Armed Forces and Society* 10 (Winter 1984).

Brigham, William J. *Guatemala: Land of the Quetzal*. London: T. Fisher Unwin, 1887.

Bureau of the American Republics. *Guatemala*. Washington, D.C.: U.S. Government Printing Office, 1892.

Burgos-Debray, Elisabeth, ed. *I . . . Rigoberto Menchu: An Indian Woman in Guatemala*. Norfolk, Va.: Thetford Press Ltd., 1983.

Burns, E. Bradford. *Eadweard Muybridge in Guatemala, 1875.* Berkeley, Calif.: University of California Press, 1986.

Calvert, Peter. *Guatemala: A Nation in Turmoil.* Boulder, Colo.: Westview Press, 1985.

Cambranes, J.C. *El Imperialismo Aleman en Guatemala.* Guatemala: Instituto de Investigaciones Economicas y Sociales de la Universidad de San Carlos de Guatemala, 1977.

Cardona, Rokael. "Descripcion de la Estructura Social y Economica en el Agro-Guatemalteco." *Politica y Sociedad* 6 (Julio–Diciembre 1978).

Carmack, Robert M. *The Quiche Mayas of Utatlan: The Evolution of a Highland Guatemalan Kingdom.* Norman, Okla.: University of Oklahoma Press, 1981.

Carter, William E. *New Lands and Old Traditons: Kekchi Cultivators in the Guatemalan Lowlands.* Gainesville, Fla.: University of Florida Press, 1969.

Cavalla Rojas, Antonio. "Guatemala en la Estrategia Militar de Estados Unidos." *Cuadernos de Marcha* Ano 2(10) (1980).

Cayetano Carpio, Salvador. *Listen, Companero.* San Francisco, Calif.: Solidarity Publications, 1983.

Centro de Investigaciones Economicas Nacionales (CIEN). *Analisis de la Situacion Economica de Guatemala, 1965–1984.* Guatemala: CIEN, 1984.

Cerezo Arevalo, Vinico. "A Talk with Guatemala's Vinicio Cerezo Arevalo." *New Leader* 66 (March 21, 1983).

Chernow, Ron. "The Strange Death of Bill Woods." *Mother Jones* 4 (May 1979).

Chincilla Aguilar, Ernesto. "El Positivismo y la Reforma en Guatemala." *Antropologia e Historia de Guatemala* 12 (1960).

Colburn, Forrest D. "De Guatemala a Guatepeor." *Latin American Research Review* 21, No. 3 (1986).

Concerned Guatemala Scholars. *Guatemala: Dare to Stuggle, Dare to Win.* San Francisco, Calif.: Solidarity Publications, n.d.

Crain, David A. "Guatemalan Revolutionaries and Havana's Ideological Offensive of 1966–1968." *Journal of Inter-American and World Affairs* 17, No. 2 (May 1975).

Davis, Shelton H., and Julie Hodson. *Witness to Political Violence in Guatemala: The Suppression of a Rural Movement.* Boston, Mass.: Oxfam America, 1982.

"Death and Disorder in Guatemala." *Cultural Survival Quarterly* 7, No. 1 (Spring 1983).

del Valle Matheu, Jorge. *Sociologia Guatemalteca.* Guatemala: Editorial Universitaria, 1950.

DiGiovanni, Jr., C. *U.S. Policy and the Marxist Threat to Central America.* Washington, D.C.: Heritage Foundation (October 15, 1980).

Early, John D. *The Demographic Structure and Evolution of a Peasant System: The Guatemalan Population.* Boca Raton, Fla.: University Presses of Florida, 1982.

Ebel, Roland H. *Political Modernization in Three Guatemalan Indian Communities.* New Orleans: Middle America Research Institute, 1969.

Estado Mayor General del Ejercito de Guatemala (General Staff). *Plan Nacional de Seguridad y Desarrollo.* Guatemala: Palacio Nacional, 1983.

Falla, Ricardo. "El Movimiento Indigena." *Estudios Centroamericanos* 33 (1978).

Fauriol, Georges, and Eva Loser. *Guatemala Election Study Report.* Washington, D.C.: Georgetown University Center for Strategic and International Studies, 1986.

Fox, Donald T. *Human Rights in Guatemala*. Geneva: International Commission on Jurists, 1979.
Frank, Luisa, and Philip Wheaton. *Indian Guatemala: Path to Liberation*. Washington, D.C.: EPICA Task Force, 1984.
Franklin, Woodman B. *Guatemala*. Oxford, Eng. and Santa Barbara, Calif.: Clio Press, 1981.
Fried, Jonathan L., Marvin E. Gettleman, Deborah T. Levenson, and Nancy Peckenham, eds. *Guatemala in Rebellion: Unfinished History*. New York: Grove Press, 1983.
Fuentes-Mohr, A. "Land Settlement and Agrarian Reform in Guatemala." *International Journal of Agrarian Affairs* 2, No. 1 (January 1955).
Fusiles y Frijoles Contra el Avance del Movimiento Popular. Hamburg: D. Hermes, 1982.
Galeano, Eduardo. *Guatemala: Occupied Country*. New York: Monthly Review, 1969.
Gallas-Quintero, Manuel. "History and Economic Theory in the Analysis of the Development of Guatemalan Indian Agriculture." Ph.D. dissertation, University of Wisconsin, 1969.
Gillespie, Richard. "Anatomy of the Guatemalan Guerrilla." *Communist Affairs* 2 (October 1983).
Gleijeses, Piero. "Guatemala: Crisis and Response." In *The Future of Central America: Policy Choices for the U.S. and Mexico*, edited by Richard R. Fagen and Olga Pellicer. Stanford, Calif.: Stanford University Press, 1983.
Gossen, Gary H. "Review of Symbolism of Subordination: Indian Identity in a Guatemalan Town." *Ethnohistory* 29 (1983).
Gott, Richard. *Guerrilla Movements in Latin America*. London: Nelson, 1970.
Grieb, Kenneth J. *Guatemalan Caudillo, The Regime of Jorge Ubico: Guatemala, 1931–1944*. Athens, Ohio: Ohio University Press, 1979.
Guerrilla Army of the Poor (EGP). "Documents from Guatemala by the Guerrilla Army of the Poor." *Contemporary Marxism* No. 3, (Summer 1981).
———. Articles from *Companero*. San Francisco, Calif.: Solidarity Publications, 1982.
Guzman Aguilar, General Carlos. "La Subversion Comunista y las Acciones Guerrilleras." *Revista de la Escuela de Comando y Estado Mayor "Manuel Enrique Araujo"* No. 18 (July–December 1970).
Guzman Bockler, Carlos, and Herbert Jean-Loup. *Guatemala: Una Interpretacion Historico-social*. Mexico: Siglo Veintiuno Editores, S.A., 1970.
Handy, Jim. *Gift of the Devil: A History of Guatemala*. Boston, Mass.: South End Press, 1984.
Herrick, Thomas R. "Economic and Political Development of Guatemala During the Barrios Period." Ph.D. dissertation, University of Chicago, 1967.
Hinshaw, Robert. *Panajachel: A Guatemalan Town in Thirty Year Perspective*. Pittsburgh: University of Pittsburgh Press, 1975.
Holleran, Mary. *Church and State in Guatemala*. New York: Columbia University Press, 1949.
Immerman, Richard. "Guatemala as Cold War History." *Political Science Quarterly* 95 (Winter 1980–81).
———. *The CIA in Guatemala*. Austin, Texas: University of Texas Press, 1983.

Inforpress Centroamericana. *Guatemala, 1984–1986.* Ciudad de Guatemala: Inforpress Centroamericana, 1984.

Institute for Mesoamerican Studies. *The Historical Demography of Highland Guatemala.* Albany, N.Y.: State University of New York, 1982.

International Human Rights Law Group (IHRLG) and Washington Office on Latin America (WOLA). *The 1985 Guatemalan Elections: Will the Military Relinquish Power?* Washington, D.C.: IHRLG and WOLA, December 1985.

James, Daniel. *Red Design for the Americas: Guatemalan Prelude.* New York: John Day, 1954.

Jenkins, Brian, and Cesar D. Sereseres. "U.S. Military Assistance and the Guatemalan Armed Forces." *Armed Forces and Society* 3, No. 4 (August 1977).

Jonas, Susanne, and David Tobis, eds. *Guatemala.* New York: North American Congress on Latin America, 1974.

Jones, Chester Lloyd. *Guatemala, Past and Present.* New York: Russell and Russell, 1966.

Karnes, Thomas L. *The Failure of Union: Central America, 1824–1960.* Chapel Hill, N.C.: University of North Carolina Press, 1961.

Kelly, Deidre. "Guatemala's Refugees: Victim and Shapers of Government Policies." *Fletcher Forum* 7 (Summer 1983).

Kennedy, Paul P. *The Middle Beat: A Correspondent's View of Mexico, Guatemala, and El Salvador.* New York: Teachers College Press, 1971.

Kinzer, Stephen, and Stephen Schlesinger. *Bitter Fruit.* New York: Doubleday Books, 1983.

Lopez Larrave, Mario. *Breve Historia del Movimiento Sindical Guatemalteco.* Guatemala: Editorial Universitaria, 1979.

MacLeod, Murdo. *Spanish Central America: A Socioeconomic History, 1520–1720.* Berkeley, Calif.: University of California Press, 1973.

Maguire, J. Robert. "The Decolonization of Belize: Self-Determination v. Territorial Integrity." *Virginia Journal of International Law* 22 (Summer 1982).

Martinez Palaez, Sero. *La Patria del Criollo.* Guatemala: Editorial Universitaria, Guatemala, 1970.

McCaughan, Susan, and Elizabeth Sutherland Matinez, eds. *Guatemala: Tyranny on Trial. Testimony of the Permanent People's Tribunal.* San Francisco, Calif.: Synthesis Publications, 1984.

McClintock, Michael. *The American Connection, Volume II: State Terror and Popular Resistance in Guatemala.* London: Zed Books, Ltd., 1985.

McCreery, David. *Development and the State in Reforma Guatemala, 1871–1885.* Athens, Ohio: Ohio University Center for International Studies, 1983.

Melville, Thomas. "The Catholic Church in Guatemala, 1944–1982." *Cultural Survival Quarterly* 7, No. 1 (1983).

Melville, Thomas, and Marjorie Melville. *Guatemala: The Politics of Land Ownership.* New York: Free Press, 1971a.

———. *Guatemala: Another Vietnam?* Harmondsworth, Eng.: Penguin Books, 1971b.

Miller, Delia, R. Seem and C. Arnson. *Background Information on Guatemala the Armed Forces and U.S. Military Assistance.* Washington, D.C.: Institute for Policy Studies, June 1981.

Miller, Herbert J. "Positivism and Educational Reforms in Guatemala, 1871–1885." *A Journal of Church and State* 8 (Spring 1966).

Millett, Richard. "The Politics of Violence: Guatemala and El Salvador." *Current History* 80 (February 1981).

———. "Guatemala: Progress and Paralysis." *Current History* 84 (March 1985).

Morley, Sylvanus, and George Brainerd. *The Ancient Maya*. Revised by Robert J. Sharer, Stanford, Calif.: Stanford University Press, 1983.

Mosk, Sanford A. "The Coffee Economy of Guatemala, 1850–1918: Development and Signs of Instability." *Inter-American Economic Affairs* 9, No. 2 (Winter 1955).

Nairn, Allan. "The Guns of Guatemala." *The New Republic* 188 (April 11, 1983).

Nanez Falcon, Guillermo. "Erwin Paul Diseldorff, German Entrepreneur in the Alta Verapez of Guatemala, 1889–1937." Ph.D. dissertation, Tulane University, 1970.

Nash, Manning. *Machine-Age Maya: The Industrialization of a Guatemalan Community*. Chicago: University of Chicago Press, 1967.

National Lawyers Guild and La Raza Legal Alliance, Joint Guatemala Delegation. *Guatemala: Repression and Resistance*. New York: National Lawyers Guild, 1980.

Naylor, Robert. "Guatemala: Indian Attitudes Toward Land Tenure." *Journal of Inter-American Studies* 9, No. 4 (October 1967).

Neier, Aryeh. "Tropic of Fire." *Mother Jones* 7 (January 1982).

Nelson, Craig W. and Kenneth I. Taylor. *Witness to Genocide: The Present Situation of Indians in Guatemala*. London: Survival International, 1983.

North American Congress on Latin American. *Guatemala: The Politics of Land Ownership*. New York: Free Press, 1971.

Organization of American States. *Report on the Situation of Human Rights in Guatemala*. Washington, D.C.: General Secretariat, Organization of American States, 1983.

Parker, Franklin D. *Travels in Central America, 1821–1840*. Gainesville, Fla.: University of Florida Press, 1970.

Pastor, Robert A. "Our Real National Interests in Central America." *The Atlantic Monthly* 250 (1982).

Payeras, Mario. *Days of the Jungle*. New York: Monthly Review Press, 1983.

Peralta, Gabriel Aguilera. "Terror and Violence as Weapons of Counterinsurgency in Guatemala." *Latin American Perspectives* 7 (Spring and Summer 1980).

Plant, Roger. *Guatemala: Unnatural Disaster*. London: Latin America Bureau, 1978.

Preston, Julia. "Guatemala: The Muffled Scream." *Mother Jones* 6, No. 9 (1981).

———. "Killing of the News in Guatemala." *Columbia Journalism Review* 20 (January–February 1982).

Raushenbush, Richard. *The Terrorist War in Guatemala*. Washington, D.C.: Council for Inter-American Security Education Institute, 1983.

Riding, Alan. "Guatemala: State of Siege." *New York Times Magazine* (August 24, 1982).

Rios Montt, Jose Efrain. *Informe al Pueblo de Guatemala*. Guatemala: Presidencia de la Republica, 1983.

Rippy, J. Fred. "Relations of the United States and Guatemala During the

Epoch of Justo Rufino Barrios." *Hispanic American Historical Review* 22 (November 1942).

Roberts, Bryan R. *Organizing Strangers: Poor Families in Guatemala City.* Austin, Texas: University of Texas Press, 1973.

Rosenthal, Mario. *Guatemala: The Story of an Emergent Latin American Democracy.* New York: Twayne Publishers, 1962.

Rubio, Casimiro. *Biografía del General Justo Rufino Barrios.* Guatemala: Tipografía Nacional, 1935.

Schneider, Ronald M. *Communism in Guatemala, 1944–1954.* New York: Praeger, 1958.

School for Advanced International Studies, Johns Hopkins University. *Report on Guatemala.* Boulder, Colo.: Westview Press, 1985.

Segesvary, Louis. *Guatemala: A Complex Scenario.* Washington, D.C.: Georgetown University Center for Strategic and International Studies, 1983.

Sereseres, Cesar D. "The Highlands War in Guatemala." In *Latin American Insurgencies*, edited by Georges Fauriol. Washington, D.C.: National Defense University Press, 1985.

Sexton, James D."Protestantism and Modernization in Two Guatemalan Towns." *American Ethnologist* 5, 1978.

———, ed. *Son of Tecun Uman: A Maya Indian Tells His Life Story.* Tucson, Ariz.: University of Arizona Press, 1981.

———. *Campesino.* Tuscon, Ariz.: University of Arizona Press, 1985.

Sexton, James D., and Clyde M. Woods. "Development and Modernization among Highland Maya: A Comparative Analysis of Ten Guatemala Towns." *Human Organization* 36 (1977).

Simons, Jean-Marie. *Guatemala: Eternal Spring, Eternal Tyranny.* New York, New York: W. W. Norton & Company, 1987.

Simons, Marlise. "Guatemala: The Coming Danger." *Foreign Policy* No. 43 (Summer 1981).

Skinner-Klee, Jorge. "La Asamblea Constituyente de 1872." *Estudios Sociales* 2 (November 1970).

Smith, Carol A. "Local History in Global Context: Social and Economic Transitions in Western Guatemala." *Comparative Studies in Society and History* 26 (April 1984).

Smith, Robert Sidney. "Indigo Production and Trade in Colonial Guatemala." *Hispanic American Historical Review* 39 (May 1959).

Spahni, Jean-Christian. *Los Indios de America Central.* Guatemala: Editorial Piedra Santa, 1981.

Stokes, Newbold, "Receptivity to Communist Fomented Agitation in Guatemala." *Economic Development and Cultural Change* 5 (July 1957).

Valle, Rafael Heliodoro. *Historia de las ideas contemporaneas en Centro America.* Mexico: Fondo de Cultura Economica, 1960.

Villacorta Calderon, Jose Antonio. *Historia de la Republica de Guatemala, 1821–1921.* Guatemala: Tipografía Nacional, 1960.

Warren, Kay B. *The Symbolism of Subordination: Indian Identity in a Guatemalan Town.* Austin, Texas: University of Texas Press, 1978.

Wasserstrom, Robert. "Revolution in Guatemala: Peasants and Politics Under the Arbenz Government." *Comparative Studies in Society and History* 17, No. 4 (1975).

Whetten, Nathan L. *Guatemala: The Land and the People.* New Haven, Conn.: Yale University Press, 1961.

White, Robert E. "Central America: The Problem That Won't Go Away." *New York Times Magazine* (July 18, 1982).

Wilkerson, S. Jeffrey K. "The Usumacinta River: Troubles on a Wild Frontier." *National Geographic* 168 (October 1985).

Wolf, Eric Robert. *Sons of the Shaking Earth*. Chicago: University of Chicago Press, 1959.

Woodward Jr., Ralph Lee. "Economic and Social Origins of the Guatemalan Political Parties (1773–1823)." *Hispanic American Historical Review* 24 (November 1965).

———. *Class Privilege and Economic Development: The Consulado de Comercio of Guatemala, 1793–1871*. Chapel Hill, N.C.: University of North Carolina Press, 1966.

———. *Central America: A Nation Divided*. 2nd ed. Oxford: Oxford University Press, 1985.

Zammit, J. Ann. *The Belize Issue*. London: Latin American Bureau, 1978.

Index